Fiesta Latina

Fiesta Latina

FABULOUS FOOD for SIZZLING PARTIES

By **RAFAEL PALOMINO**

with **ARLEN GARGAGLIANO** Photographs by **ANASTASSIOS MENTIS**

CHRONICLE BOOKS
SAN FRANCISCO

Library of Congress Cataloging-in-Publication Data available.

ISBN 0-8118-4410-2

Manufactured in China.

Designed by Ayako Akazawa
Prop styling by Laurent Laborie
Food styling by Megan Fawn Schlow
Typesetting by Blue Friday Type & Graphics and Janis Reed
From the photographer: Special thanks to my mother, Eleni Mentis.

Distributed in Canada by Raincoast Books
9050 Shaughnessy Street
Vancouver, British Columbia V6P 6E5

10 9 8 7 6 5 4 3 2 1

Chronicle Books LLC
85 Second Street
San Francisco, California 94105

www.chroniclebooks.com

Dedication

This book is dedicated to the memory of my best friend, Alberto Frías, who made every moment a *fiesta latina*.

Acknowledgments

Many thanks to my terrific writer, Arlen Gargagliano; my agent, Jane Dystel; my editor, Bill LeBlond, along with Amy Treadwell and the staff at Chronicle Books; my Chronicle publicity manager, Michael Weisberg; and my staff at Pacífico and Sonora.

6

Introduction

You can feel the warmth as soon as you enter. Embraces and soft kisses welcome you into the party. You're greeted with a wave of music, animated conversations, and the enticing aroma of food. Sparkling with people, brimming with all kinds of treats and *tragos* (drinks), there is nothing like *una fiesta latina!* Trays of gorgeous bite-size appetizers are passed throughout the room; and side tables are adorned with bowls of fresh vegetable and fruit salsas; serving platters of tamales, empanadas, and ceviches; and assortments of marinated and grilled skewers of chicken, beef, lobster, and shrimp.

The bar—colorful with Passion Fruit Caipirinhas, Coconut Mojitos, and Pomegranate Margaritas—buzzes with laughter. Amidst a backdrop of music that provokes slight hip swinging, fingers reach to choose from the platters of grilled Sugarcane Shrimp Skewers with Jalapeño Coconut Sauce; Ropa Vieja Duck Dumplings; and Sonora Tostones with Pacífico Garlic Herb Mojito. The smiles say it all: *la fiesta latina* is sunshine, electricity, and, *por supuesto* (of course), fabulous flavors.

I've loved throwing parties for a long time. When I was growing up in Colombia, my parents and family enjoyed the giving—and receiving—that comes from hosting numerous events, from cocktail parties and Sunday afternoon dinners to special-occasion fiestas like birthdays, anniversaries, and weddings. I guess I've got that party-giving gene, which is probably what prompted me to get into the restaurant business in the first place! In both of my Port Chester, New York, restaurants, as well as in my New Haven restaurant, and my new place in Greenwich, Connecticut, and through Pasión, my catering company, I continue to throw many, many parties. But I also play host at home, with the help of my wife and our two children, who are now old enough to assist—and enjoy—the whole party process.

So how do you make a party Latin-style? There are some basic steps I follow, whether I'm prepping for an off-premises party that I cater, for an event in one of my restaurants, or for a gathering in my own home. I always tell the hosts that by following these steps, they can—as they should—enjoy the pre-party process as well as the party. Organization is key: write lists—and read them! (Whenever we cater a party, there are lists posted in the kitchen so that we all—chefs, helpers, and wait staff—can refer to them as needed.) I strongly urge you to do the same. After all, the adrenaline that hosts feel prior to their guests' arrival should be from excitement and anticipation, not from the stress of having forgotten some important piece of the party prep.

First and foremost, there's the menu. Choose dishes that match your party in terms of time of day. For example, if it's a brunch, you may want to serve the Pacífico Lobster and Scrambled Egg Wrap, along with Colombian Arepas de

Choclo with Guacamole. You could complement those appetizers with ceviches, like the Chilean Salmon and Pomegranate Ceviche, or even the Blood Orange, Shrimp, and Mango-Wasabi Ceviche. Lobster Chipotle Crabcakes, or the Sirloin Steak, Ají Amarillo, and Shiitake Mushroom Spring Rolls would make equally welcome additions to your menu, with which I would include cocktails like Mango Caipiroskas, and perhaps Pomegranate Margaritas. Of course, an early-evening cocktail party—or a Saturday night dinner party— would most likely have a different choice of dishes and cocktails.

The weather will also be a deciding factor in your menu. For example, if it's a steamy summer day, go with a cooling ceviche—like my Watermelon, Shrimp, and Jalapeño Chile Ceviche, maybe the Charred Yellow Tomato and Cilantro Gazpacho, and some grilled appetizers like the Sugarcane Shrimp Skewers with Jalapeño Coconut Sauce, or the Marinated Lobster Tail and Scallop Pinchos. Serve with thirst-quenching Mojitos—like the Coconut or Pineapple Mojito. If it's a chilly day, choose warming treats like Arroz Moro, Chipotle Potato Cheese Gratin, some quesadillas, or my Vegetable Paella. Accompany with cocktails like Noches de Cartagena, whose heart of *aguardiente* will certainly bring some heat to the fiesta!

Next, try to prepare as much as you can ahead of time. The individual recipes contain suggestions for doing this. Advance preparation alleviates a lot of last-minute stress—and helps you enjoy the fiesta, too! Once you've decided on your menu, you can create a shopping list and then systematically prep each item accordingly.

Also, you need to think about the mood of the party. Choose table settings, serving dishes and plates, flowers, and music to match the *ambiente,* or ambience, you want to create. Colorful tablecloths, along with candles, scattered petals or leaves, and central floral arrangements help to create a scene. Find fun umbrellas or stirrers for your cocktails. Select music—or live musical entertainment—that reflects what you want your guests to feel. These little *toques,* or touches, contribute a great deal to the whole success of the party.

Here's my advice. Read through this book with an eye for exploration. Don't be afraid to try different recipe combinations. Find dishes that stimulate your imagination—and palate. Experiment by making them for your immediate family and friends before making them for a larger group. Once you start to feel comfortable with a dish, add your own touches to make it your own. Don't be afraid to delve into something new—that's how we chefs have discovered some of our greatest successes!

When I think about what makes a party *una fiesta latina*, I think of things that make people feel welcome. The celebration should reach out to your guests and gently pull them in by sensually conveying comfort and warmth; it needs to make guests feel that they are where they should be at that point in time. When your guests are happy, and you are happy, you've succeeded. *¡Qué disfruten!* Enjoy!

JUST AS IMPORTANT AS A FIRST IMPRESSION,

chapter

1 Appetizers

AREPAS AND OTRAS
PASABOCAS

APPETIZERS SET THE SCENE FOR YOUR FIESTA. VARIED, COLORFUL, AND delicious, your choice of *pasabocas* should excite you. This chapter contains a selection of several of my favorites, from sweet corn Arepas de Choclo, or Colombian corncakes, to the slightly smoky, sparky, and embracing Chipotle Potato Cheese Gratin. Read through them, find something that attracts you, and try it!

Colombian Arepas de Choclo with Guacamole

MAKES ABOUT 18 AREPAS AND 2½ CUPS GUACAMOLE   This combination of food tells the story of my life! *Arepas,* Colombian griddled Johnny cakes, were probably my first food. The manchego cheese, a Spanish cheese that adds depth to the *arepas,* represents my Mediterranean experience as a young man living and working in Europe. The guacamole, inspired by my visits to Mexico as well as by the influences of many of my current kitchen staff members, is a salsa that I now enjoy virtually every day. Together these ingredients combine to make one of my favorite cocktail appetizers. You can make the *arepas* ahead of time and then prepare the guacamole the morning of your party and sauté the *arepas* just before serving them. Of course, you'll want to let them cool just to room temperature before topping them with the guacamole.

GUACAMOLE

4 ripe Hass avocados, peeled, seeded, and coarsely chopped

1 medium red onion, diced

¼ cup chopped cilantro, plus additional leaves for garnish

1 teaspoon chipotle purée (see page 138) or Tabasco sauce (or according to taste)

1 teaspoon kosher salt

2 medium yellow tomatoes, roasted (see page 135) and cut into ⅛-inch dice

Juice of ½ lime

AREPAS

2 cups fresh or thawed frozen corn kernels

1½ cups chicken stock (page 128) or water, heated

2 cups yellow *harina precocida* (instant cornmeal)

2 tablespoons sour cream

1 tablespoon sugar

2 ounces manchego (or white Cheddar) cheese, grated

2 tablespoons unsalted butter

Prepare the guacamole: Place the avocados, onion, and chopped cilantro in a large glass or ceramic bowl, and toss well; the avocado will get mushy. Add the chipotle or Tabasco, salt, tomatoes, and lime juice and stir until well blended. Serve immediately, or cover tightly and refrigerate for up to 1 day.

Prepare the *arepas*: In a blender, process the corn kernels and chicken stock until smooth. Pour the *harina precocida* into a large bowl. Stir in the sour cream and sugar. Pour in the chicken-stock-and-corn mixture while stirring with your hands or a wooden spoon. Add the grated cheese. Form the mixture into a ball. Divide into 8 pieces. Roll each piece into a ball, and then flatten it into a pancake about ¼ inch thick and 2 inches in diameter (rub your fingers around the edge so that it maintains its thickness). At this point you can cover the *arepas* with a damp kitchen towel and refrigerate them for up to 1 day before sautéing.

Melt 1 tablespoon of the butter in a medium sauté pan (or on a sandwich press) over medium heat. Sauté the *arepas,* in batches if necessary, until golden, 3 to 5 minutes on each side. (Add more butter to the pan as needed.) They should be toasted on the outside but soft in the middle. Let cool to room temperature, top with the guacamole, garnish with the cilantro leaves, and serve immediately.

Lobster Chipotle Crabcakes

MAKES 4 CRABCAKES   Crabcakes—easily picked up and eaten—are perfect for parties. This recipe, which requires very little prep time, will yield fabulous results. You can prepare them the morning of your party and sauté them just before your guests arrive.

2 lobster claws (2 ounces lobster meat), cooked (see page 133), shelled, and chopped

4 ounces jumbo lump crabmeat

2 green onions, white and light green parts only, thinly sliced

2 tablespoons Chipotle Sour Cream (page 129)

1 teaspoon minced chives, plus additional chives cut into ½-inch strips for garnish

Kosher salt

¼ cup crushed yuca or malanga chips (such as Terra Chips, available in large supermarkets)

Canola oil for sautéing

4 teaspoons Mango, Jalapeño, and Radish Salsita (page 133)

In a large bowl, combine the lobster, crabmeat, green onions, and Chipotle Sour Cream. Use your hands to mix. Add the chives and salt to taste. Pour the crushed yuca chips into a plate. Shape the lobster-and-crabmeat mixture into four 2-inch cakes. Roll the cakes in the crushed yuca chips.

Heat about ¼ cup oil in a medium sauté pan over a medium flame. Sauté the crabcakes until golden on both sides, 3 to 5 minutes per side. Drain on paper towels and serve immediately, topped with about a teaspoon of the salsita and garnished with chives.

Watermelon Martini, page 124

Passion Fruit and
Foie Gras Napoleons

MAKES 2 SERVINGS   Sometimes you're just in the mood for a party of two; this recipe is perfect for those times. This seductive recipe—for those who love the rich flavors of foie gras that balance so beautifully here with the sweet corn *arepas*—is a wonderful way to start a chilly evening. So when it gets frosty outside, get the fire going inside, make a couple of Passion Fruit Caipirinhas (page 121), and settle in for your fabulous treats.

AREPAS

1 cup yellow *harina precocida*
   (instant cornmeal)

½ cup hot water, or more as needed

1 tablespoon sour cream

1 teaspoon sugar

1 tablespoon grated white Cheddar cheese

SALSITA

¼ cup roasted (see page 139), diced ripe
   sweet plantains

2 tablespoons unsweetened passion fruit
   purée (available in Latin American
   and large supermarkets)

2 tablespoons diced mango

1 tablespoon diced fresh pineapple

1 teaspoon chopped shallot

3 pinches mâche, plus 2 pinches
   when assembling

1 pinch minced chives

1 teaspoon unsalted butter

1 ounce foie gras, cold and firm (you may
   want to freeze it for 10 minutes), sliced
   into two 2-inch spheres

: : *continued*

Prepare the *arepas:* Combine the *harina precocida* with the ½ cup hot water in a large bowl. Use your hands to mix well. Add more hot water as needed; it should form a ball of dough. Add the sour cream, sugar, and Cheddar cheese. Using a rolling pin, roll the dough out about ¼ inch thick. Using a 2-inch round cookie cutter, cut the dough into 4 rounds. Set aside.

Make the salsita: In a medium bowl, combine the plantains, passion fruit purée, mango, pineapple, shallot, 3 pinches mâche, and chives, and mix well. Set aside.

In a medium sauté pan over medium heat, melt the butter and sauté the *arepas* until golden, about 2 minutes on each side. Set aside. Wipe out the pan with a paper towel. Sauté the 2 pieces of foie gras until golden, about 1½ minutes on each side. Set aside.

Assemble the napoleons: Place one *arepa* on a serving plate. Top with a slice of foie gras, then another *arepa,* a pinch of mâche, and a spoonful of salsita. Spread the salsita around the plate. Repeat to make a second napoleon. Serve immediately.

Yuca Frita

MAKES 12 TO 15 APPETIZER SERVINGS It's amazing how many people I've won over from French fries to yuca fries! Like French fries, these *bocaditos* are easy to eat. Customers and party guests alike enjoy the sweet meat of yuca inside a crisp crust, dipped into a variety of salsas. Here I serve them with my saffron, thyme, and garlic mojito, but you can also try them with Ají Verde (page 127), Sofrito (page 136), or even ketchup! I like to serve these with ice-cold Negra Modelo beer (a Mexican beer), or with Pomegranate Margaritas (page 120).

6 pounds frozen yuca, preferably
    Costa Rican

8 to 10 cups chicken stock (page 128),
    canned broth, or water

Canola oil for deep-frying

Kosher salt

Pacífico Garlic Herb Mojito (page 28;
    optional)

Put the yuca in a large stockpot and add chicken stock to cover by 2 inches; you'll need to check the stock and keep it at this level. Bring to a boil, reduce the heat, and simmer, uncovered, until tender, about 30 minutes. Remove the yuca from the stock with a slotted spoon, and let drain. Using your fingers, remove the string from the cores of the yuca.

Preheat the oven to 250°F and place one or two ovenproof serving platters inside. Cut the yuca into ½-inch-thick slices. In a deep, heavy pot or deep-fryer, heat 2 inches of oil to 365°F. Fry a small batch of yuca slices until lightly browned, 3 to 5 minutes. Use a slotted spoon or skimmer to transfer the yuca to paper towels to drain. Once drained, place the yuca in a large bowl, add salt to taste, and toss lightly. Transfer to the platters in the oven. Repeat until you've fried all the remaining yuca. Serve immediately, with or without the mojito for dipping.

Niçoise Olives and Goat Cheese Lamb Anticucho Style

MAKES 8 CHOPS   When my wife and I moved from Manhattan to Bedford, New York, I welcomed not only the tranquil setting, but also the opportunity to throw barbecues in my backyard. This dish was born on a sunny Sunday afternoon when I had guests coming over for a late-afternoon cocktail party. I marinated the chops for about 2 hours (while we had cocktails and played soccer in the backyard) and then quickly grilled them. The salad of greens, niçoise olives, tomatoes, and anchovies is gorgeous and delicious. Since then, I've adapted the recipe for the restaurant, where it's met with equally positive acclaim.

½ rack lamb chops, cut into eight ¼-inch-thick chops

Paprika Garlic-Herb Marinade (page 81)

1 handful frisée lettuce

2 small bundles mâche

2 vine-ripened tomatoes, coarsely chopped

¼ cup niçoise olives, pitted and coarsely chopped

Kosher salt and freshly ground pepper

8 white anchovies, diced

½ sweet plantain, roasted (see page 139) and diced

½ cup olive oil

¼ cup white balsamic vinegar

8 French Bread Croutons (page 131)

3 ounces goat cheese

8 sprigs thyme

Whole chives, for garnish

Purple potato chips (such as Terra Chips, available in large markets), for garnish

Marinate the lamb chops in the marinade for 1 to 2 hours. Heat an outdoor grill to high, or use a grill pan. Grill the lamb chops until medium-rare, about 3 minutes on each side.

Meanwhile, in a large bowl, combine the frisée, mâche, tomatoes, and olives. Add salt and pepper to taste. Stir in the anchovies and sweet plantain and set aside.

:: *continued*

Niçoise Olives and Goat Cheese Lamb Anticucho Style

In a small bowl, whisk together the olive oil and balsamic vinegar. Pour one-fourth of this dressing on the salad. Toss the croutons in the salad, but then remove them and set on the serving platter. Surround the croutons with the salad mixture. Add remaining dressing according to taste.

Preheat the broiler to high. Place the lamb chops on a baking sheet for broiling. Spoon about 1 teaspoon of goat cheese on top of each lamb chop. Sprinkle the leaves from a sprig of thyme on top of each chop. Broil until the cheese begins to melt, about 1 minute. Remove from the pan, and place the chops on top of the croutons on the serving platter. Stand the chives upright in the goat cheese for garnish, and decoratively spread the purple potato chips over the salad mixture. Serve immediately.

Chipotle Potato Cheese Gratin

MAKES 8 TO 10 APPETIZER SERVINGS   My year in southern France introduced me to a wealth of new dishes and flavors; the potato gratin is one that I have adored since my first bite. Whether I serve it at parties in my own home or in my restaurants, guests and customers alike sing the praises of this slightly sparky and smoky version of the French classic. Easy to prepare, this dish can be an appetizer, a side dish, or even a lunch. At home I like to let guests help themselves, so I usually place this gratin on a sideboard next to a Sonora Caesar and Anchovy Salad (page 103).

2 pounds Idaho potatoes, peeled and very thinly sliced

1¼ cups crema agria (see page 139), crème fraîche, or heavy cream

2 small cloves garlic, minced

2 teaspoons chipotle purée (see page 138), or to taste

1 cup grated manchego, Gruyère, or Swiss cheese

2 tablespoons finely chopped cilantro

Preheat the oven to 350°F. Grease a 6-cup baking dish with butter and arrange half of the potatoes in a layer in the dish. In a small bowl, combine the crema agria, garlic, and chipotle purée. Mix well. Spread evenly on top of the potatoes. Sprinkle half the cheese on top. Repeat with the remaining potatoes, cream mixture, and cheese. Bake, uncovered, until the top is golden brown and the potatoes are tender, about 1 hour. If the potatoes are brown after 50 minutes, put aluminum foil—buttered on one side to prevent sticking—on top so that they don't overcook. Let the gratin rest for 10 minutes before serving. Sprinkle with cilantro and serve.

Sonora Charred Yellow Tomato and Cilantro Gazpacho

MAKES 4 APPETIZER SERVINGS Gazpacho, the Andalusian-born chilled soup, boasts the cool flavors of summer-fresh garden vegetables. This liquid salad was apparently quite different at birth; rumor holds that it was originally made with just bread, water, and olive oil! The most popular contemporary versions of this fabulous soup contain three ingredients found in abundance in Andalusia: ripe tomatoes, olive oil, and garlic. This Nuevo Latino interpretation adds the delectable tones of roasted tomatoes, red onion, and fresh cilantro leaves. Serve well chilled, in small dishes with crumbled garlic-toasted baguette slices sprinkled on top. Although this blended soup is thirst-quenching on its own, it's also good when complemented by a dry Spanish sherry.

3 yellow beefsteak tomatoes, grilled (see page 135)

1 red onion, roasted (see page 135)

2 plum tomatoes, chopped

2 teaspoons roasted garlic paste (see page 135)

1 bunch cilantro, stemmed and coarsely chopped

2 cups tomato juice

¼ cup white balsamic vinegar

¼ cup olive oil

Kosher salt and freshly ground pepper

Crumbled French Bread Croutons with garlic (page 131) for garnish

In a large food processor fitted with a steel blade, combine the yellow tomatoes, onion, plum tomatoes, and garlic paste. Add the cilantro, tomato juice, vinegar, and oil, and process until almost smooth. Add salt and pepper to taste. Transfer to a large bowl and chill in the refrigerator for at least 1 hour (or overnight). Serve topped with the crumbled garlic croutons.

Sonora Tostones with Pacífico Garlic Herb Mojito

MAKES ABOUT 12 TOSTONES AND 1 CUP MOJITO   Found in the Dominican Republic, Cuba, and Puerto Rico, these twice-fried plantains make a great appetizer or side dish. Though they're a bit messy, they're perfect party fare. My customers especially enjoy their *tostones* gently bathed in this thyme-saffron butter sauce and served with Pineapple Mojitos (page 120) or Brazilian Cosmopolitans (page 123).

MOJITO

¾ cup dry white wine

Juice of 1 lime

Pinch of saffron threads

Pinch of salt

5 cloves roasted garlic (see page 135)

1 cup (8 ounces) cold unsalted butter, cut into small cubes

Leaves from 2 sprigs thyme

2 large unripe (green) or barely ripe (slightly yellow) plantains

About 1 cup canola oil for frying

Kosher salt and freshly ground pepper

Prepare the mojito: In a medium stainless-steel pan, combine the wine and lime juice and bring to a boil. Lower the heat to moderate. Add the saffron and salt and simmer until the sauce is slightly reduced, 2 to 3 minutes. Add the roasted garlic cloves, and smash them with the whisk so that they become part of the sauce. Add the butter slowly, stirring constantly with the whisk. Once you've added the butter, stir in the thyme leaves and set aside. (If the sauce breaks, simply process it in a blender to bring it back to a unified, creamy sauce.) If you're not going to be frying the plantains immediately, you can keep the mojito warm by pouring it into a thermos; just stir before serving.

Fry the plantains: Using a sharp knife, slice the ends from each plantain. Cut a lengthwise slit, and peel them by hand. Cut each one into 1-inch-thick slices, on the diagonal.

Heat about 1 inch of oil in a large, heavy sauté pan over medium heat. When the oil is hot enough to make a plantain slice sizzle, start frying the plantains in batches. Cook until golden, but not too browned, about 3 minutes on each side. Transfer to paper towels to drain. (Be sure to reserve the oil—you'll be using it again.)

Cover the *tostones* with a clean kitchen cloth and use your body weight to press down and smash them. When they are flattened, reheat the oil over moderate heat. Fry the plantains again, in batches, until they are golden, about 2 minutes on each side. Drain, and add salt and pepper to taste. Top with the mojito (or you can toss them into a bowl with the mojito and mix them until they're well bathed), and serve immediately.

Pacífico Lobster
and Scrambled Egg Wrap

MAKES 2 WRAPS (8 APPETIZER SERVINGS) When we started serving brunch at Pacífico, I wanted to create a menu of breakfast items with a Latino flair—and still keep with our seafood theme. This wrap has been a consistently popular item. Easy to make and serve, it is perfect brunch finger food!

½ cup cooked chopped lobster meat (see page 133), fresh, canned, or thawed frozen

1 stalk celery, finely diced

½ red onion, finely diced

2 tablespoons mayonnaise

Juice of ½ lime

Kosher salt and freshly ground pepper

4 eggs

2 burrito-size flour tortillas

1 teaspoon Chipotle Garlic Mayonnaise (page 129)

Chopped chives, for garnish

Combine the lobster, celery, red onion, and mayonnaise in a medium bowl. Mix well. Add the lime juice and salt and pepper to taste. Set aside, or cover and refrigerate for 1 to 3 hours.

In a small bowl, beat the eggs until well blended. Pour into a large nonstick sauté pan and cook, stirring frequently, over moderate heat until done. Remove from the heat, and combine with the lobster salad.

Place half of the mixture along the center of a tortilla in a horizontal line. Roll up the tortilla so that it's in a cigar shape. Use a sharp knife to cut it into 4 slices, and stand the slices up vertically. Repeat with the remaining tortilla and lobster mixture. Top each slice with just a bit of the Chipotle Garlic Mayonnaise and a sprinkle of chives. Serve immediately.

chapter

2

Flour Tortilla Sandwiches and Asian-Inspired Turnovers

DIFFERENT, THEY DO SHARE CERTAIN ATTRIBUTES; FOR EXAMPLE, THEY CAN BOTH easily embrace a variety of flavors and textures. From the simple Lobster and Avocado Quesadilla to the more exotic Ropa Vieja Duck Dumplings, this small treasure chest of appetizers is sure to have something to inspire you.

Lobster and Avocado Quesadilla with Guacamole

MAKES 1 QUESADILLA, 4 PIECES   Whether it's an afternoon snack for *mis hijos*, my children, a cocktail party with friends on a sunny summer afternoon, or a late-night treat with cocktails at the bar, quesadillas are great—versatile and *delicioso*. I promise that these will be a popular addition to your party repertoire. Remember, you can always vary the ingredients depending on your *gusto*, or taste. This recipe can be multiplied depending on the number of guests you are serving.

1 teaspoon vegetable oil

2 tablespoons guacamole (page 132)

Two 6-inch flour tortillas

¼ cup chopped cooked lobster meat (see page 133). fresh, canned, or thawed frozen

½ cup grated Cheddar cheese

Chipotle Sour Cream (in a squeeze bottle), for garnish (page 129)

Preheat the oven to 450°F. Heat the oil in a medium sauté pan over medium heat. Spread 1 tablespoon of the guacamole on one side of one of the tortillas and evenly distribute the lobster and Cheddar cheese on top. Cover with the other tortilla. Place in the heated pan and let brown for about 30 seconds. Flip and brown the other side. Immediately place on a baking sheet and bake in the preheated oven for 2 minutes, or until the cheese melts. Remove from the oven, cut into quarters, and garnish with a squeeze of sour cream. Divide the remaining tablespoon of guacamole among the wedges, placing a dab in the center of each.

Coconut Mojito, page 122

Roasted Duck
Ropa Vieja Quesadillas

MAKES 4 QUESADILLAS, 16 PIECES   The literal translation of *ropa vieja* is "old clothes"; this is what shredded meat resembles! *Ropa vieja*—typically made with beef—is a popular dish throughout Latin America. This Nuevo Latino interpretation of a quesadilla uses the hearty flavor of duck, balanced here with the taste of roasted red peppers and creamy goat cheese.

About ½ cup canola oil

8 duck legs (to yield a total of 1 cup cooked, shredded duck meat)

Kosher salt and freshly ground pepper

1 carrot, coarsely chopped

1 onion, coarsely chopped

3 tablespoons tomato paste

1 cup dry red wine

3 stalks celery, coarsely chopped

4 bay leaves

4 sprigs thyme

1 sprig rosemary

1 tablespoon whole black peppercorns

1 to 2 cups chicken stock (page 128) or canned, low-salt chicken broth

1 red onion, finely diced

1 cup thinly sliced green onions, white and light green parts only

1 teaspoon ground cumin

1 teaspoon garlic salt

1 teaspoon sweet paprika

½ cup chopped pitted kalamata olives

2 teaspoons minced fresh ginger

2 teaspoons soy sauce

2 red bell peppers, roasted (see page 135), and finely diced

Eight 6-inch flour tortillas

4 ounces goat cheese

Preheat the oven to 350°F. Pour about 2 tablespoons of the canola oil into a flame-proof roasting pan and place over medium-high heat. Season the duck legs with salt and pepper and add to the pan. Sauté until golden. Remove the duck legs and drain some of the fat from the pan. Add the carrot and onion. Add the tomato paste and continue cooking until the carrot is lightly browned and tender, 8 to 10 minutes.

: : *continued*

Pour in the red wine and scrape up the cooked pieces from the pan with a wooden spoon. Add the celery, bay leaves, thyme, rosemary, and black peppercorns. Add the duck again, pour in enough chicken stock just to cover the legs, and bring to a boil. Cover with foil, and place in the oven. Bake until tender and cooked through, about 2½ hours. Remove from the pan and turn the oven off. When cool enough to handle, skin and shred the meat into bite-size pieces. Set aside.

Meanwhile, in a medium sauté pan, heat 4 tablespoons of the canola oil. Add the red onion, green onions, cumin, garlic salt, and paprika. Stir in the olives, ginger, soy sauce, and roasted red peppers. Add the shredded duck to the mixture. Stir to mix and remove from the heat.

Lay 4 tortillas out on a work surface. Spread 1 ounce of goat cheese on each tortilla. Divide the shredded duck mixture among the tortillas, spreading it evenly. Top with the remaining tortillas.

Preheat the oven to 350°F. Heat about 1 tablespoon oil in a nonstick sauté pan over medium heat. Place a filled tortilla in the pan and cook until lightly browned, about 30 seconds on each side. Place on a baking sheet. Repeat with the remaining tortillas. Place in the oven until the cheese starts to melt, about 1 minute. Remove and cut each quesadilla into 4 wedges. Be very careful not to burn yourself with the hot cheese! Place on a serving dish, and serve immediately.

Shrimp, Roasted Pepper, and Tetilla Cheese Quesadillas

MAKES 6 QUESADILLAS, 24 PIECES   Tetilla, a Spanish cheese, comes from Galicia, which is in the northwest of Spain. Its distinct shape—resembling a Hershey's Kiss—is what gives it the name *tetilla* (literally translated as "nipple"). The flavor of tetilla cheese is clean and smooth, and it melts beautifully, making it a perfect quesadilla cheese.

1 cup cooked shrimp, diced

½ cup diced roasted red bell pepper
(see page 135)

1 cup grated tetilla or white Cheddar cheese

1 tablespoon cilantro

Kosher salt and freshly ground pepper

Twelve 6-inch flour quesadillas

1 tablespoon canola oil

1½ beefsteak tomatoes, sliced (you should
have 6 slices, 1 per quesadilla)

In a medium bowl, combine the shrimp and bell pepper. Stir in the cheese and cilantro. Add salt and pepper to taste.

Lay 6 tortillas out on a work area. Divide the shrimp and cheese mixture among the tortillas, spreading it evenly. Top with the other 6 tortillas.

Heat the oil in a large sauté pan over medium heat. Sauté each tortilla pair until browned and the cheese is melting, 1 to 2 minutes on each side. Be careful not to burn yourself with the cheese! Open each tortilla top and place a tomato slice in the center. Cut each quesadilla into 4 wedges, and serve immediately.

Shrimp and Portobello Teriyaki Dumplings

MAKES ABOUT 32 DUMPLINGS   There's a fortune-cookie mystique about dumplings. After all, you're never quite sure what you'll get until you bite into one! I welcome the challenge of creating dumplings that match ideal taste, texture, and cultural combinations—here, for example, you've got elements from the Far East, the Mediterranean, and Latin America. When we prepare these in the restaurant, I use the thinner wontons, which I buy in Chinatown. If you can't get to Chinatown, find a vendor that sells a lot of them (so that you can be sure that they're fresh). You can serve these dumplings in covered bamboo steamers lined with banana leaves, with small dishes of the Ginger Soy Dipping Sauce, or on larger platters with several ramekins of the sauce. Either way, I'm sure your guests will enjoy these little packages as much as my customers do.

DIPPING SAUCE

1 cup soy sauce

5 tablespoons brown sugar

1 cup water

1 tablespoon minced fresh ginger

2 tablespoons lemongrass, coarsely chopped (optional)

DUMPLINGS

1 pound medium shrimp, peeled and deveined

2 tablespoons olive oil

1 tablespoon minced fresh ginger

2 shallots, minced

1 clove garlic, minced

3 cups finely diced, stemmed, and cleaned portobello mushrooms

½ cup white wine

⅓ cup soy sauce

3 tablespoons rice vinegar

1 tablespoon honey

½ teaspoon dark sesame oil

1 mango, peeled, pitted, and cut into ¼-inch dice

2 green onions, white and light green parts only, thinly sliced

2 red bell peppers, roasted (see page 135), and finely diced

Kosher salt and freshly ground pepper

2 tablespoons chopped cilantro

6 egg whites, plus 4 for "gluing" wontons

1 package wonton wrappers (about 50)

Prepare the dipping sauce: Combine the soy sauce, brown sugar, water, ginger, and lemongrass (if desired) in a medium saucepan and bring to a boil over medium-high heat. Lower the heat and simmer until the mixture is reduced by half, about 20 minutes. Strain. Serve immediately, or cover and refrigerate for up to 5 days.

Prepare the dumplings: Steam ¼ pound of the shrimp until lightly pink, about 1 minute. Set aside, and then chop finely.

Heat the oil in a large sauté pan over medium heat. Add the ginger, shallots, and garlic and sauté for 1 minute. Add the mushrooms and wine, and cook for an additional 4 minutes, or until dry. Remove from the heat. Add the soy sauce, rice vinegar, honey, and sesame oil. Stir in the mango, green onions, roasted pepper, salt and pepper to taste, and cilantro. Add the steamed shrimp and set aside.

Meanwhile, in a food processor, combine the remaining raw shrimp and egg whites. Process until it becomes a fine paste. Fold into the mushroom mixture. Lay single wonton wrappers out on a flat, clean surface. Spoon 1 heaping tablespoon of the mixture onto the center of the wrapper. Wet the borders of the wonton square with egg white (you can use your finger). Fold the dumpling into a triangular shape and seal the top point by pressing. Then open up the sides, and seal 4 more corners (so that you have a 5-pointed dumpling). Make sure the wonton wrapper is sealed; use egg white as needed. Repeat until you've filled all the wrappers.

Bring water to a full boil in a heavy pot. Using a long spoon, gently place the dumplings into the boiling water, and boil until the wrappers are cooked (like cooked pasta, they shouldn't feel sticky to the touch), 3 to 5 minutes. In the restaurant, we put a wire strainer in the pot to hold the dumplings and then lift them out. You can do that, or use a slotted spoon to remove them. Be gentle! They're very delicate. Serve the dumplings as soon as they are ready, with the dipping sauce.

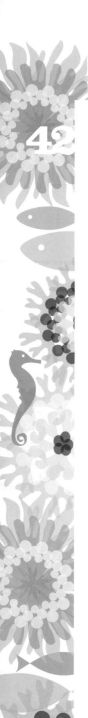

Ropa Vieja Duck Dumplings

MAKES 8 DUMPLINGS   I love to take my family for dim sum at one of the many wonderful restaurants in New York's Chinatown. My children especially enjoy choosing their dumplings—which come with all sorts of fillings—and dipping them in sauce before devouring them. My recipe for steamed dumplings, inspired by the Chinese classics, has components of my Colombian heritage and my Mediterranean experience. Since I've introduced these to my patrons at Sonora, in Port Chester, New York, they've been one of the most requested appetizers. Once you get into the swing of making them—and eating them—I'm sure you'll agree.

DUMPLINGS

1 duck leg

1 tablespoon vegetable oil

1 tablespoon minced red onion

½ green onion, white part only, diced

1 teaspoon finely minced fresh ginger

1 teaspoon chopped fresh thyme

1 tablespoon diced roasted red bell pepper
  (see page 135)

1 tablespoon soy sauce

1 teaspoon chopped cilantro

½ teaspoon ground cumin

½ teaspoon chili powder

6 kalamata olives, pitted and chopped

4 medium fresh shiitake mushrooms,
  julienned

8 wonton wrappers

1 egg white

DIPPING SAUCE

Juice of ½ lime (2 tablespoons)

2 tablespoons water

1½ ounces panela, crushed (available
  in Latin American markets), or
  3 tablespoons dark brown sugar

2 tablespoons white balsamic vinegar

2 tablespoons soy sauce

1 teaspoon minced fresh ginger

Prepare the dumplings: Bring a medium saucepan full of water to a boil. Simmer the duck leg until tender, about 45 minutes. Remove from the water, let cool to the touch, and shred into bite-size pieces. Set aside.

Meanwhile, prepare the rest of the filling. Heat the oil in a medium sauté pan over medium heat, and add the red onion, green onion, ginger, thyme, and roasted pepper. Stir in the soy sauce, cilantro, cumin, chili powder, olives, and mushrooms, and cook for 5 to 7 minutes. Add the shredded duck, mix well, and remove from the heat.

Take one of the wonton wrappers and place it in the palm of your hand. Add a heaping tablespoon of the duck mixture. Wet the borders of the wonton square with the egg white (you can use your finger). Fold the dumpling into a triangular shape and seal the top point by pressing. Then open up the sides, and seal 4 more corners (so that you have a 5-pointed dumpling). Make sure the wonton wrapper is sealed; use egg white as needed. Repeat with the remaining filling and wrappers.

Prepare the dipping sauce: Combine the lime juice, water, panela, vinegar, soy sauce, and ginger in a medium saucepan. Bring to a boil, stirring constantly, and cook until the panela is totally dissolved, about 4 minutes. Use immediately, or cover and refrigerate for up to 5 days.

Cook the dumplings: Bring water to a full boil in a heavy pot. Using a long spoon, gently place the dumplings into the boiling water, and boil until the wrappers are cooked (like cooked pasta, they shouldn't feel sticky to the touch), 3 to 5 minutes. In the restaurant, we put a wire strainer in the pot to hold the dumplings and then lift them out. You can do that, or use a slotted spoon to remove them. Be gentle! They're very delicate. Serve the dumplings as soon as they are ready, with the dipping sauce.

chapter

3

Citrus Marinated Fish and Peruvian-Style Sashimi

SNACK THAT CONSISTS OF RAW FISH "COOKED" BY CITRUS JUICES, IS THOUGHT TO have been born in either Peru or Ecuador. *Tiraditos* are the result of the fabulous culinary marriage of Japanese and Peruvian cuisine *(la cocina nikkei)*. Made of thin, carpaccio-like slices of fish, not unlike sashimi, *tiraditos* are seasoned according to *sabor peruano,* or Peruvian taste. Now popular throughout the Americas, ceviches and *tiraditos* are made zesty thanks to a variety of chiles—like ají amarillo, poblano, jalapeño, and many more. Whenever I prepare a party—either at one of the restaurants or elsewhere—I always suggest a ceviche assortment because it has something for everyone. From the Watermelon, Shrimp, and Jalapeño Chile Ceviche, ideal for those who are just starting to dabble in the ceviche world, to the Sirloin Steak Tiradito with Traditional Chimichurri, perfect for those who crave a light fix of meat gently drizzled with South American pesto, I'm sure you'll find something that piques your palate.

Yellowfin Tuna and Coconut Poblano Ceviche

MAKES 6 APPETIZER SERVINGS   This silky ceviche is the perfect treat for a steamy summer afternoon. To add extra zing to this starter, serve spicy Pepper Potato Chips alongside (page 134).

12 ounces sashimi-grade yellowfin tuna fillets, skinned and cut into ¼-inch dice

Juice of 2 lemons

Juice of 2 limes

Juice of 2 oranges

1 medium-size red onion, finely diced

1 red bell pepper, seeded and finely diced

2 poblano chiles, roasted (see page 135), peeled, seeded, and diced

2 tablespoons coarsely chopped cilantro

One 14-ounce can coconut milk

3 tablespoons cream of coconut

1 tablespoon honey

Kosher salt and freshly ground pepper

Put the tuna in a large glass or ceramic bowl. Add the citrus juices, mix well, and cover tightly. Add the remaining ingredients, stir to mix, and refrigerate until the tuna is turning opaque on the outside but is still rare on the inside, about 15 minutes. Serve chilled.

Blood Orange, Shrimp, and Mango-Wasabi Ceviche

MAKES 6 APPETIZER SERVINGS   Cuernavaca, the sunny Mexican mountain-nestled city, was aptly named "city of eternal spring" by the Aztecs. It was here, several years ago, that I had the ceviche that inspired me to create this one. Serve it in a martini glass with chips, or in half a fresh coconut.

Sections from 3 blood oranges (tangerines or regular oranges can also be used)

2 mangos, peeled, pitted, and diced

Juice of 1 blood orange

Juice of 6 regular oranges

Juice of 2 limes

2 tablespoons finely diced red onion

1 tablespoon diced chives

2 tablespoons white balsamic vinegar

1½ pounds cooked shrimp, peeled and deveined

1 teaspoon wasabi powder

Kosher salt and freshly ground black pepper

Fresh chives, cut into 2- to 3-inch pieces, for garnish

In a large ceramic or glass bowl, combine the juice from the orange sections, the mangos, orange juices, lime juice, onion, chives, and vinegar. Add the shrimp, wasabi powder, and salt and pepper to taste. Cover and let sit at room temperature for half an hour. Garnish with the chives and serve immediately.

Pineapple Mojito, page 120

Yellowfin Tuna and Papaya Tiradito

MAKES 6 TO 8 APPETIZER SERVINGS   There is something intoxicating about the marriage of fresh papaya and tuna. With a light kiss of roasted jalapeño vinaigrette, this fruit and fish combination is simply dazzling. Pacífico customers constantly rave about this appetizer, which is both elegant and easy to prepare. You can make the vinaigrette days before your party and bring it back to room temperature to serve with your fresh papaya and tuna.

VINAIGRETTE

1 papaya, seeded and diced into
    large chunks

1 jalapeño chile, roasted (see page 135),
    halved, and seeded

½ cup white balsamic vinegar

1 clove garlic, chopped

1 medium shallot, chopped

5 sprigs cilantro

Kosher salt and freshly ground pepper

¼ cup water

½ cup olive oil

1 pound sashimi-grade yellowfin tuna,
    wrapped tightly in plastic (into a roulade)
    and frozen hard (for at least 6 hours or
    overnight)

1 large papaya, seeded

Prepare the vinaigrette: Combine the papaya, jalapeño, vinegar, garlic, and shallot in a blender. Add the cilantro, salt and pepper to taste, and water. Slowly add the olive oil and purée until blended. Let sit for about 15 minutes. Use immediately, or cover and refrigerate for up to 5 days. Bring to room temperature and put into a squeeze bottle prior to serving.

Using a professional slicer, slice the frozen tuna on setting 2, so that your slices are very thin. Then slice the papaya (using the slicer or a very sharp knife) into rounds or slices that match the tuna slices. On a large platter (or on small plates), arrange the slices of tuna and papaya so that they slightly overlap. Drizzle the vinaigrette on top of the slices. Serve with cocktail forks.

Chilean Sea Bass
Margarita Ceviche

MAKES 6 APPETIZER SERVINGS   Named after the classic Mexican cocktail, this tequila-kissed ceviche, delicate and flavor packed, will leave you with a smile. Serve in chilled martini glasses.

8 ounces Chilean sea bass fillets, skinned and cut into thin (⅛-inch-thick) slices

Juice of 6 oranges

Juice of 6 limes

¼ cup superfine sugar, or to taste

½ cup José Cuervo tequila

1 medium-size jalapeño chile, very thinly sliced (using a mandoline, if possible)

1 red onion, halved and thinly sliced into strips

½ cup chopped cilantro

Kosher salt and freshly ground pepper

Put the sea bass slices in a large glass or ceramic bowl. Add the citrus juices, sugar, tequila, jalapeño, and onion. Mix well. Cover tightly and refrigerate for at least 20 minutes (but not longer than 45 minutes or it will be overcooked). Stir in the cilantro and salt and pepper to taste just prior to serving.

Watermelon, Shrimp, and Jalapeño Chile Ceviche

MAKES 4 APPETIZER SERVINGS   Everybody loves the sweet summertime taste of watermelon. Refreshing and tender, it blends perfectly with the citrus flavors, as well as with the cooked shrimp and the delicate spark of jalapeño. You can make the citrus mixture ahead of time and then simply add the slightly undercooked shrimp 15 minutes before you're ready to serve the dish, to allow it to "cook" through. For the melon chunks, which add color, style, and texture to this ceviche, I like to use an oval fluted melon baller.

Juice of 5 oranges

Juice of 2 limes

1 cup fresh watermelon juice (made by puréeing watermelon in a blender), plus ½ cup watermelon balls

3 tablespoons white balsamic vinegar

1½ jalapeño chiles, finely diced

6 medium shrimp, peeled, lightly blanched, and butterflied

10 fresh mint leaves, stacked, rolled, and cut into fine shreds, plus additional mint leaves for garnish

½ red onion, thinly julienned

1 cup puréed roasted red bell peppers (see page 135)

Kosher salt and freshly ground pepper

Combine the citrus juices, watermelon juice, vinegar, and jalapeños. Add the shrimp and shredded mint and let sit for 15 minutes. Stir in the red onion, roasted peppers, and salt and pepper to taste. Add the watermelon balls. Serve in chilled martini glasses, garnished with fresh mint leaves.

Chilean Salmon and Pomegranate Ceviche

MAKES 4 APPETIZER SERVINGS   Pomegranate juice adds color and depth to this ceviche. The kiss of coconut cream adds balance, while the toasted coconut adds crunch. Try it with Pomegranate Margaritas (page 120) at your next cocktail party.

Juice of 2 oranges

Juice of 2 limes

1 ripe mango, peeled, pitted, and finely diced

1 cup pomegranate juice

8 ounces sashimi-grade salmon, cut into ½-inch pieces

1 tablespoon coconut mixture (page 130)

1 teaspoon toasted coconut (see page 137), for garnish

Combine the citrus juices, mango, and pomegranate juice in a medium bowl. Cover and refrigerate for at least an hour, or overnight. Fifteen minutes prior to serving, add the salmon. Serve in chilled martini glasses, drizzled with the coconut mixture and topped with toasted coconut.

Passion Fruit Caipirinha, page 121

Kumamoto Oysters with Beet and Cucumber Mignonette

MAKES 18 APPETIZER SERVINGS   Kumamoto is the name of the large bay on Kyushu, the southernmost island of Japan, which is where these oysters originated. Now grown in oyster farms from California to Washington, these sweet, beautiful, and plump oysters are my absolute favorite! I enjoy the fact that they're creamy and briny. Serve these for a special brunch or cocktail party with Mango Mimosas—which are easily prepared by combining 6 ounces of champagne with 2 ounces of mango nectar.

18 Kumamoto oysters, scrubbed

½ cup finely diced roasted beets (see page 134)

½ cup finely diced peeled Japanese (seedless) cucumber, or seeded English or garden cucumber

½ shallot, minced

1½ tablespoons white balsamic vinegar

¼ teaspoon kosher salt

⅛ teaspoon freshly ground black pepper

½ cup champagne

¼ teaspoon prepared horseradish

Open the oysters and discard the top shell. Combine the remaining ingredients in a bowl and mix well. Arrange the oysters on a platter. Using a teaspoon, spoon a little mignonette on the tip of each oyster shell. (You also have the option of leaving the mignonette in a small bowl and letting guests serve themselves.) Serve immediately.

Lobster, Mango, Ginger, and Lemongrass Ceviche

MAKES 6 APPETIZER SERVINGS   This fabulous sweet-and-sour ceviche has attributes beyond its great taste. You can prepare the lobster and the sauce ahead of time, and then blend them together so that the lobster finishes cooking in the citrus juices just before your guests arrive.

1 tablespoon minced fresh ginger

1 tablespoon honey

½ stalk lemongrass, coarsely chopped

Juice of 2 lemons

Juice of 2 limes

Juice of 2 oranges

¼ cup excellent-quality mango purée

¼ cup white balsamic vinegar

4 quarts water

Four 1-pound lobsters

¼ cup dry white wine

2 tablespoons coarsely chopped cilantro

1 red bell pepper, seeded and finely diced

Kosher salt and freshly ground pepper

In a medium bowl, combine the ginger, honey, and lemongrass. Add the citrus juices. Stir in the mango purée and balsamic vinegar. Let sit for half an hour and then strain.

In a large saucepan, bring the water to a boil. Add the lobster and wine. Cook until the shells turn bright red, about 3 minutes. (You want to undercook them because they will continue to cook in the citrus juices.) Transfer the lobsters to bowls of ice water until cool to the touch. (At this point you can cover and refrigerate them overnight.)

Remove the lobster meat from the shells and chop into ½-inch chunks. Transfer to a large glass or ceramic bowl. Add the citrus sauce and mix well. Stir in the cilantro and red bell pepper. Add salt and pepper to taste. Cover tightly and refrigerate for at least 30 minutes, or up to 1 hour. Stir the mixture well before serving.

Pomegranate Margarita, page 120

Sun-Dried Tomato and Shrimp Ceviche

MAKES 4 TO 8 APPETIZER SERVINGS   Colorful, tart, and refreshing, this ceviche is great with an ice-cold beer! You can prepare the shrimp ahead of time and combine it with the remaining ingredients at least 15 minutes (or up to 30 minutes) before serving.

16 large shrimp, lightly blanched, peeled, and cut into ½-inch chunks

Juice of 4 oranges

Juice of 4 limes

Juice of 4 lemons

6 tablespoons Sun-Dried Tomato Chimichurri (page 137)

¾ teaspoon honey

2 handfuls frisée lettuce, coarsely chopped into 1-inch chunks

2 tablespoons chopped cilantro

Combine the shrimp and citrus juices in a large bowl. Stir in the chimichurri and the honey and mix well. Add the lettuce and cilantro. Let sit for about 15 minutes, and serve in martini glasses.

Pineapple and
Mint Salmon Ceviche

MAKES 4 APPETIZER SERVINGS   When we decided to begin serving brunch at Pacífico, there were dishes that naturally called out to be on the menu, and this was one of them. Fresh pineapple juice—along with the bright flavors of citrus juices and the rich flesh of salmon—make this ceviche a great choice for a sleepy Sunday brunch.

1½ cups fresh pineapple juice

Juice of 3 limes

Juice of 2 oranges

1 cup diced fresh pineapple

1 tablespoon sugar

5 fresh mint leaves, stacked, rolled, and cut into fine shreds for garnish

Kosher salt and freshly ground pepper

12 ounces sashimi-grade salmon, cut into thin slices

Combine all the ingredients except for the salmon in a large bowl. Cover and refrigerate for at least an hour or overnight. Fifteen minutes prior to serving, add the salmon. Serve in chilled martini or wine glasses.

Niçoise and Cilantro Yellowfin Tuna Tiradito

MAKES 6 TO 8 APPETIZER SERVINGS   Infused oils add pleasure to food. I sometimes use them as an alternative to spices and herbs. They not only add
flavor to fish, meat, and vegetables, they also can be a great base for
dressings, sauces, and marinades. Here a light brush of oil adds a kiss of
flavor to the tasty tuna meat.

OIL

1 shallot, coarsely chopped

1 clove garlic

¼ cup chopped cilantro

1 cup olive oil

2 tablespoons coarsely chopped pitted
    niçoise olives

Leaves from 1 sprig thyme

1 pound sashimi-grade yellowfin tuna,
    wrapped tightly in plastic (into a roulade)
    and frozen hard (for at least 3 hours
    or overnight)

½ cup fresh lime juice

Kosher salt and freshly ground pepper

¼ cup coarsely chopped cilantro

Prepare the oil: Combine the shallot, garlic, cilantro, olive oil, olives, and thyme in
a blender and process just until smooth. Use immediately, or cover and keep for several months in the refrigerator. Return to room temperature and stir before serving.

Thinly slice the tuna, using a slicer set at 2 or a very sharp knife. Arrange the tuna
slices on plates or a single platter, so that they just slightly overlap. Drizzle the lime
juice on top. Brush the oil over the tuna. Sprinkle with salt and pepper to taste, and
with the cilantro. Serve immediately.

Sirloin Steak Tiradito with Traditional Chimichurri

MAKES 6 TO 8 APPETIZER SERVINGS This simple and ultra-sexy appetizer is for people who appreciate great meat—and subtlety. Make sure you buy excellent-quality sirloin steak. Prepare the chimichurri ahead of time, and then bring it to room temperature just before serving. Serve the remaining chimichurri with chips, or use it as a marinade or dipping sauce on another night. I like to pass this appetizer around with cocktail forks so that guests can serve themselves.

CHIMICHURRI

3 cloves garlic

Leaves from ½ bunch cilantro

Pinch of kosher salt

½ cup white balsamic vinegar

1½ cups olive oil

9 ounces sirloin steak, wrapped tightly in plastic wrap and frozen for at least 3 to 4 hours

1 tablespoon chopped chives, for garnish

Freshly ground pepper

Make the chimichurri: Combine the garlic, cilantro, salt, and balsamic vinegar in a blender and pulse until mixed. Slowly pour in the olive oil. Pour into a squeeze bottle to use immediately, or cover and refrigerate for up to 10 days.

Using a professional slicer, slice the frozen meat on 2, so that it's quite thin. Spread the slices on a platter so they just slightly overlap. Using a squeeze bottle, gently drizzle the chimichurri so that there's a bit on each piece of meat. Sprinkle with chives and freshly ground pepper to taste, and serve immediately.

chapter

4

Thin Flour Pastries and Savory Turnovers

WITH A GREAT ASSORTMENT OF SAVORY TREATS, HAVE BEEN A PART OF MY EATING and cooking repertoire for as long as I can remember, spring rolls are a relatively recent—and very successful—adoption. The Yellowfin Tuna, Coconut, and Asian Black Rice Rolls were an immediate hit; the luscious tuna, silky coconut, and slightly nut-flavored black rice, wrapped in a light spring-roll envelope, work together to arouse even the sleepiest of taste buds. The more traditional Colombian Sirloin and Cumin Empanadas, topped with *ají verde,* our Colombian version of guacamole, are probably one of the most requested appetizers in my restaurants and at parties. This assortment of treats will stimulate you— and your guests!

Quinoa and Sweet Plantain Spring Rolls

MAKES 2 ROLLS OR 8 APPETIZER SERVINGS I grew up with empanadas—the savory and sweet pastry pockets that can be found in various forms throughout the Americas. Like many dishes in Nuevo Latino cooking, these rolls are an example of a traditional dish reinvented with a slightly different touch. In this case, it's an Asian twist. Most of the ingredients in the filling would be typical in an empanada. I like the freshness the seaweed wrap has to offer. It also works nicely with the fresh tropical fruits and lettuce; the flavors are clean and bright.

1 cup cooked quinoa (see page 140)

2 tablespoons julienned mango

2 tablespoons finely diced fresh pineapple

½ red bell pepper, roasted (see page 135) and julienned

Kosher salt and freshly ground pepper

1 tablespoon toasted coconut (see page 137)

1 tablespoon chopped chives

½ ripe plantain, roasted (see page 139) and diced

1 tablespoon white balsamic vinegar

1 tablespoon coarsely chopped pitted niçoise olives

2 sheets nori (Japanese dried and pressed seaweed sheets, available in large markets)

2 leaves frisée lettuce

In a medium bowl, combine the quinoa, mango, pineapple, and red pepper. Add salt and pepper to taste. Stir in the coconut, chives, roasted plantain, vinegar, and olives.

Set the 2 sheets of nori on a work surface. Spread the quinoa mixture evenly on the bottom three-fourths of each sheet, leaving about an inch at the top. Place a leaf of frisée in the center of each. Starting at the bottom, roll up the nori, using your fingertips, so that it looks like a large cigar. When you get to the top, moisten the edge so that the roll stays sealed.

Using a very sharp knife, cut each roll into 4 sections. Turn so they're vertical, and serve immediately.

Yellowfin Tuna, Coconut, and Asian Black Rice Rolls

MAKES 8 APPETIZER SERVINGS   Asian lore says that rice will calm your nerves, lift your depression, and make your body stronger. I find that using this gorgeous dark purple rice adds a wonderful visual and flavorful balance to the rich coconut and luscious yellowfin tuna in this Nuevo Latino tapa. The *aji amarillo*—an excellent complement to the rice, fish, and coconut combo— adds a bit of spark. Serve with Pineapple or Coconut Mojitos (pages 120, 122).

⅔ cup cooked black rice (see page 127)

2 tablespoons julienned mango

2 teaspoons cream of coconut

4 teaspoons toasted coconut (see page 137)

4 teaspoons coconut milk

6 ounces thinly sliced sashimi-grade yellowfin tuna, thinly sliced

½ teaspoon *aji amarillo* (see page 138)

Kosher salt and freshly ground black pepper

2 heaping teaspoons finely diced fresh pineapple

2 sheets nori (Japanese dried and pressed seaweed sheets, available in large markets)

In a large bowl, mix together all ingredients except the nori. Stir until well blended. Place the nori sheets in front of you, and evenly spread the black rice mixture on the bottom three-fourths of them, leaving just about an inch at the top. Starting at the bottom, roll up the nori, using your fingertips, so that it looks like a large cigar. When you get to the top, moisten the edge so that the roll stays sealed.

Using a very sharp knife, cut each roll into 4 sections. Turn so they're vertical, and serve immediately.

Oyster Mushroom and Eggplant Empanadas with Habanero Sauce

MAKES 12 MEDIUM EMPANADAS The ingredients in these empanadas represent the time I spent studying and working in southern France, while the sauce—along with the dough—reflects my experience as a child in Colombia, along with the Nuevo Latino cooking style I've developed here in New York. All these ingredients work beautifully together to create a taste treat that my customers have come to crave. The habanero sauce has a bit of spark; it excites the flavors of the empanadas and adds a rich brick-red color to the backdrop of the white turnovers. When we make this particular size of empanadas, we use a dough press, a handy tool that you can easily find in specialty and kitchenware shops. The press not only creates uniform empanadas, it also crimps the edges for you, so that each one looks gorgeous. (However, if you don't have a dough press, see page 74 for tips on how to handle the dough.)

FILLING

1 tablespoon unsalted butter

½ teaspoon minced garlic

1 cup diced oyster mushrooms

1 cup diced peeled eggplant

1 cup diced roasted red bell peppers
    (see page 135)

½ cup diced pitted niçoise or kalamata olives

Kosher salt and freshly ground pepper

½ cup chopped cilantro

Pinch of ground cumin

½ cup goat cheese

Pinch of fresh thyme leaves

DOUGH

2 cups white *harina precocida*
    (instant cornmeal)

2 cups warm water

Kosher salt

SAUCE

3 shallots, roasted (see page 135)

2 plum tomatoes, roasted (see page 135)

1½ habanero chiles, roasted (see page 135),
    seeded, and coarsely chopped

½ cup white balsamic vinegar

Pinch of paprika

Pinch of ground cumin

¼ cup canola oil

2 cloves roasted garlic (see page 135)

Kosher salt and freshly ground pepper

Canola oil for deep-frying

Prepare the filling: Heat the butter in a medium sauté pan over medium heat. Add the garlic, mushrooms, and eggplant. Cook until the eggplant starts to soften, 8 to 10 minutes. Add the roasted peppers, olives, salt and pepper to taste, cilantro, and cumin and cook for just a couple of minutes longer. Remove from the heat. Stir in the goat cheese and thyme. Set aside.

Prepare the dough: Put the *harina precocida* in a large bowl. Fill a large spouted cup with the warm water, and gradually pour it into the bowl. Add salt to taste and mix well with your hands. The dough will feel slightly sticky and elastic. Cover it and refrigerate for 10 minutes to set. Line a work surface with a sheet of plastic wrap. Place the dough on top of the plastic, and cover with another sheet. Using a rolling pin, roll the dough out to a thickness of ⅛ inch. Keeping the plastic wrap on top, use a wide jar or a 5-inch-diameter biscuit or cookie cutter to cut rounds of dough.

Take off the top layer of plastic wrap and remove the dough between the rounds. Place a dough circle into a 4⅞-inch dough press. Place 1 tablespoon of the filling in the bottom half of the circle. Press to seal. Repeat for each empanada. Reroll the remaining dough and make additional empanadas until you've used up the filling. (If you have extra dough, you can make small pancakes and fry them in butter!) At this point you can cook the empanadas or keep them, covered with damp kitchen towels and plastic wrap, in the refrigerator for up to 2 days.

Prepare the sauce: Combine the shallots, tomatoes, chiles, vinegar, paprika, cumin, oil, garlic, and salt and pepper to taste in a blender and process until blended. Set aside, or cover and refrigerate for up to 5 days. Heat the sauce prior to serving.

Cook the empanadas: In a deep, heavy pot or deep-fryer, heat 2 to 3 inches of oil to 365°F. Fry the empanadas, a few at a time, until lightly browned and puffed, about 3 minutes on each side. Using a skimmer, transfer to a wire rack set on a baking sheet. Serve immediately, or let cool and freeze for up to 3 months. Reheat in a preheated 350°F oven until heated through, about 25 minutes. Serve with the warm sauce either drizzled on top or in a separate dish for dipping.

Colombian Sirloin and Cumin Empanadas with Ají Verde

MAKES ABOUT 24 EMPANADAS Empanadas—dough turnovers made in different shapes and sizes and with different fillings, found all over Latin America—are always party favorites. These two-bite-size pastries go with just about everything. This version is not so quick to make, but it is certainly worth the effort, *y te prometo,* I promise you, they will go quickly! Plus you can make them ahead of time and freeze them. Depending on the crowd you have, you may want to double the recipe. For each restaurant order (four empanadas), I serve a small bowl of Ají Verde (page 127), which is easily scooped up with the empanada; you should plan to make enough ají verde for the empanadas—and more to serve as a dip.

FILLING

1 cup peeled diced potatoes (¼-inch dice)

1 tablespoon olive oil

2 cups diced sirloin steak (¼-inch dice)

½ cup finely chopped green onions

1 cup seeded and diced plum tomatoes

2 teaspoons ground cumin

DOUGH

2 cups yellow *harina precocida* (instant cornmeal)

2 cups warm water

Kosher salt

Canola oil for deep-frying

½ cup Ají Verde (page 127)

Prepare the filling: Put the diced potatoes in a medium saucepan and cover with plenty of cold salted water. Cover, bring to a boil, and cook until tender, about 8 minutes. Drain and set aside. Meanwhile, in a large sauté pan or skillet, heat 1 tablespoon of olive oil over medium-high heat. Add the sirloin and cook, stirring occasionally, until browned, about 5 minutes. Stir in the green onions and tomatoes and cook for 2 minutes. Add the cooked potatoes and cumin and cook for 3 minutes, stirring occasionally. Transfer to a bowl and set aside.

: : *continued*

Prepare the dough: Put the *harina precocida* in a large bowl. Fill a large spouted cup with the warm water, and gradually pour it into the bowl. Add salt to taste and mix well with your hands. The dough will feel slightly sticky and elastic. Cover and refrigerate for 10 minutes to set. Line a work surface with a sheet of plastic wrap. Place the dough on top of the plastic, and cover with another sheet. Using a rolling pin, roll the dough out to a thickness of ⅛ inch. Keeping the plastic wrap on top, use a 2½-inch-diameter biscuit or cookie cutter to cut rounds of dough.

Take off the top layer of plastic wrap and remove the dough between the rounds. Set aside. Place 1 heaping teaspoon of the filling on the bottom half of each circle. Use the plastic wrap to fold the circles over. Seal the edge with your moistened finger. Repeat for each empanada. Reroll the remaining dough and make additional empanadas until you've used up the filling.

Cook the empanadas: In a deep, heavy pot or deep-fryer, heat 2 to 3 inches of canola oil to 365°F. Fry the empanadas, a few at a time, until lightly browned and puffed, about 3 minutes on each side. Using a skimmer, transfer to a wire rack set on a baking sheet. Serve immediately, or let cool and freeze for up to 3 months. Reheat in a preheated 350°F oven until heated through, about 25 minutes. Serve with Ají Verde.

Sirloin Steak, Ají Amarillo, and Shiitake Mushroom Spring Rolls

MAKES 7 ROLLS *Fritanguerías colombianas*—like my favorite one outside the famous Campin Stadium in Bogotá—are heavenly for those of us who grew up in Bogotá. As a teen, I'd often go there with friends after the games and munch out on *empanadas de chorizo* (sausage) and yuca, each served with a different *ají,* or sauce. The flavors in this spring roll represent my sweet memories, and my new influences.

1 tablespoon unsalted butter

5 medium shiitake mushrooms, cut less than ½ inch long (including stems)

1 shallot, finely diced

4 green onions, white and light green parts only, finely diced

8 ounces diced cooked sirloin steak

½ cup golden raisins

1 tablespoon chopped cilantro

1 teaspoon *ají amarillo* (available at Latin American groceries)

7 spring roll skins

Canola oil for deep frying

Preheat the oven to 250°F. In a medium sauté pan over medium heat, melt the butter. Sauté the mushrooms and shallot until the mushrooms start to soften, about 2 minutes. Add the green onions. Remove the sauté pan from the heat and stir in the steak, raisins, cilantro, and *ají amarillo.*

Place a spring roll skin, on the diagonal, on a work surface in front of you. Spoon about 2 tablespoons of the mixture in the center of the spring roll skin, and spread it into a line. Wet the borders of the roll with water (using your finger). Roll the wrapper up diagonally, folding in the sides. Repeat until all the spring rolls are made.

In a deep, heavy pot or deep-fryer, heat 2 inches of oil to 375°F. Add the spring rolls, one at a time, and fry, without crowding them, turning constantly so they cook evenly, until golden brown and crisp, usually less than a minute. Remove with a strainer or slotted spoon and drain on paper towels. Keep them warm in the oven. You can freeze the rolls once they have cooled. To serve, defrost, arrange on a rack placed on a baking sheet, and reheat in a preheated 375°F oven until crisp, about 15 minutes.

Chipotle Crabmeat and Sweet Plantain Empanadas

MAKES ABOUT 16 EMPANADAS   Empanadas, to the chef, are like blank canvases to a painter; they allow for play and exploration with myriad combinations of flavors, textures, and colors. Here I've used the empanada backdrop to house one of my favorite flavor combinations: sparky chipotle, smooth crabmeat, and sweet plantains. Easy to store and reheat, these savory treats are great for making ahead of time and baking as your guests arrive.

FILLING

2 cups jumbo lump crabmeat

2 sweet plantains, roasted (see page 139) and diced

2 green onions, white and light green parts only, finely chopped

1½ teaspoons chipotle purée (see page 138)

1 cup diced mango

Kosher salt

DOUGH

2 cups yellow or white *harina precocida* (instant cornmeal)

2 cups warm water

Kosher salt

Canola oil for deep-frying

Prepare the filling: In a large bowl, combine the crabmeat, sweet plantains, green onions, and chipotle purée. Add the diced mango and salt to taste. Cover and refrigerate until ready to use.

Prepare the dough: Put the *harina precocida* in a large bowl. Fill a large spouted cup with the warm water, and gradually pour it into the bowl. Add salt to taste and mix well with your hands. The dough will feel slightly sticky and elastic. Cover and refrigerate for 10 minutes to set. Line a work surface with a sheet of plastic wrap. Place the dough on top of the plastic, and cover with another sheet. Using a rolling pin, roll the dough out to a thickness of ⅛ inch. Keeping the plastic wrap on top, use a wide jar or a 5-inch-diameter biscuit or cookie cutter to cut rounds of dough.

Take off the top layer of plastic wrap and remove the dough between the rounds. Set aside. Place 1 heaping teaspoon of the filling on the bottom half of each circle. Use the plastic wrap to fold the circles over. Seal the edge with your moistened finger. Repeat for each empanada. Reroll the remaining dough and make additional empanadas until you've used up the filling.

Cook the empanadas: In a deep, heavy pot or deep-fryer, heat 2 to 3 inches of oil to 365°F. Fry the empanadas, a few at a time, until lightly browned and puffed, about 3 minutes on each side. Using a skimmer, transfer to a wire rack set on a baking sheet. Serve immediately, or let cool and freeze for up to 3 months. Reheat in a preheated 350°F oven until heated through, about 25 minutes.

AS MUCH AS I LOVE EATING PASABOCAS, BITE-SIZE

chapter

5

Main Dishes, Rice, Salads, and Shellfish

PLATOS FUERTES, ARROZ, ENSALADA, Y MARISCOS

APPETIZERS, I ALSO LOVE HAVING—AND OFFERING—THE OPTION OF HEARTIER fare. Easily rested on a sideboard, dishes like Palomino's Vegetable Paella, brimming with fresh plum tomatoes, baby spinach, shiitake mushrooms, roasted red peppers, and kalamata olives, all with a backdrop of saffron-golden rice, calls diners with their fragrant aroma and alluring beauty. Equally irresistible are skewers of lobster tail or shrimp; the Sugarcane Shrimp Skewers with Jalapeño Coconut Sauce, which combine the sweet taste of grilled shrimp, the spark of jalapeño, and the light tropical touch of coconut, are sure to dazzle your guests. Find your own favorite combos and create a feast that includes an assortment of dishes.

Grilled Skirt Steak with Yuca and Chorizo Hash Browns

MAKES 8 SERVINGS An important part of the *parillada mixta* (mixed grilled meats) in Colombia and Argentina, skirt steak is tender and succulent. This version, marinated in a paprika garlic-herb sauce, is ideally cooked on a grill. When combined with the hash browns, it makes a Latin-style meat-and-potatoes meal that is perfect hearty fare for a fall fiesta.

PAPRIKA GARLIC-HERB MARINADE

2 teaspoons chopped fresh thyme

½ teaspoon ground cumin

1 teaspoon Spanish paprika

½ teaspoon chili powder

1 teaspoon garlic salt

2 teaspoons minced garlic

1 cup vegetable oil

½ teaspoon ground black pepper

4 pounds skirt steak, cut into 8 equal pieces

Kosher salt and freshly ground pepper

HASH BROWNS

2 tablespoons canola oil

2 teaspoons minced garlic

1 cup fresh corn kernels

1 cup diced plum tomato

½ cup diced green onions, white and pale green parts only

½ teaspoon ground cumin

1½ cups quartered shiitake mushrooms

1½ cups diced chorizo (Colombian or Spanish)

1½ cups diced fried yuca (follow instructions on page 21, but dice the yuca prior to deep-frying it)

1 cup chicken stock (page 128), canned low-salt chicken broth, or water

Kosher salt and freshly ground pepper

½ cup Pacífico Garlic Herb Mojito (page 28)

Sprigs of cilantro for garnish

: : *continued*

Prepare the marinade: Combine the thyme, cumin, paprika, chili powder, garlic salt, garlic, oil, and ground pepper in a large container; mix until well blended. Marinate the skirt steak for 8 hours or overnight. Sprinkle both sides with salt and pepper.

Prepare the hash browns: Heat the oil in a large sauté pan over medium heat and cook the garlic until it is a light cinnamon color, about 30 seconds. Add the corn, tomato, and green onions, followed by the cumin, mushrooms, chorizo, and fried yuca. Add the chicken stock and cook until heated through, about 5 minutes. Add salt and pepper to taste.

Cook the steaks: Heat a grill to high. Grill the skirt steaks for about 2 minutes on each side. Remove, let sit for a moment, and cut slits about ½ inch apart (not cutting all the way through), so that you can fan out each serving of meat on a plate. To serve, add the hash browns, and drizzle the meat with the mojito. Garnish with cilantro sprigs.

Roasted Chicken and Saffron-Lobster Mashed Potatoes

MAKES 6 SERVINGS One of my favorite comfort foods, roasted chicken is always a great party dish! The Chardonnay Peanut Sauce blends beautifully with the marinated chicken, as well as with the soft and fabulously flavored mashed potatoes.

MARINADE

1½ cups chicken stock (page 128) or low-salt chicken broth

½ cup julienned dry-packed sun-dried tomatoes, soaked in hot water for 20 minutes

1 teaspoon olive oil

1 cup minced red onion

1 tablespoon fresh rosemary leaves

1 tablespoon roasted garlic (see page 135)

Kosher salt and freshly ground pepper

½ teaspoon annatto powder

1 teaspoon paprika

¼ cup chopped cilantro

3 boneless free-range chickens, 3½ pounds each, split in half

MASHED POTATOES

6 large Idaho potatoes, peeled and quartered

6 cups chicken stock (page 128) or canned low-salt chicken broth

1 teaspoon kosher salt

1 tablespoon unsalted butter

½ cup heavy cream, at room temperature

½ teaspoon roasted garlic (see page 135)

Few threads of saffron

½ cup cooked lobster meat (see page 133), diced

6 slices manchego cheese

CHARDONNAY PEANUT SAUCE

4 cups chardonnay

1 tablespoon minced shallot

2 tablespoons creamy peanut butter

2 cups coconut milk

¼ cup cream of coconut

2 cups chicken stock (page 128) or canned low-salt chicken broth

1 tablespoon chopped chives, for garnish

1 tablespoon diced seeded plum tomato, for garnish

1 tablespoon chopped roasted peanuts, for garnish

: : continued

Roasted Chicken and Saffron-Lobster Mashed Potatoes

Prepare the marinade: Pour the chicken stock into a medium saucepan. Combine the sun-dried tomatoes with the olive oil. Add both to the saucepan, along with the onion, rosemary, and garlic. Stir in salt and pepper to taste, annatto, and paprika, bring to a boil and cook for 5 minutes. Let cool and add the cilantro before pouring into a food processor fitted with a steel blade or a blender; process until smooth. Coat the chicken with the marinade. Cover and refrigerate for 8 hours or overnight.

Make the mashed potatoes: Place the potatoes in a large pot. Add the chicken stock, cover, and bring to a boil. Cook for 20 to 30 minutes, until the potatoes are very soft. Drain well, and return the potatoes to the pot or to the bowl of an electric mixer with a paddle attachment (not a food processor). Add the salt, butter, cream, garlic, and saffron, and mash until very smooth. Add the lobster. If you are mashing by hand, change to a whisk toward the end to fluff out the potatoes. Keep warm until ready to serve.

Roast the chicken: Preheat the oven to 450°F. In a medium sauté pan over medium-high heat, sear the chicken halves on all sides until golden, about 5 minutes per side. Immediately place the chicken on a baking sheet and roast in the oven until cooked through, 12 to 15 minutes. Preheat the broiler, place a slice of manchego cheese on top of each half, and broil the chicken, in batches if necessary, until the cheese melts, about 30 seconds.

Prepare the sauce: While the chicken is roasting, in a medium saucepan, over medium-high heat, cook the wine and shallot until reduced by half, 10 to 12 minutes. Add the peanut butter, coconut milk, cream of coconut, and chicken stock. Bring to a boil, whisking frequently. Cook until all ingredients are well blended. Use immediately.

Set a chicken half on each plate. Sprinkle the chives, tomato, and peanuts on top. Spoon some of the mashed potatoes next to the chicken. Drizzle the chicken with the sauce. Serve immediately.

Thanksgiving Turkey with Chorizo and Apple Stuffing

MAKES 30 TO 35 SERVINGS   Although we all have our favorite Thanksgiving recipes, it's often great fun to venture out into new territory. I encourage you to celebrate your next Thanksgiving with this very simple yet scintillating dish. My Thanksgiving customers always love this turkey and stuffing. The beer, paprika, garlic-herb, and cumin flavors—which can be overpowering on their own—meld richly into a flavoring that is truly Latino, and a great complement to the natural turkey flavor. The stuffing—a marriage of chorizo, cornbread, and apple—balances the soft turkey meat, adding a delightful melange of textures and flavors. Baking the stuffing separately makes it easier for you to prep. You can even cook the stuffing the day before and then reheat it just before serving.

Double recipe of Paprika Garlic-Herb Marinade (page 81)

2 turkeys, 18 pounds each, preferably organic, washed and giblets removed

3 bottles of Aguila (Colombian) beer, or any light beer

STUFFING

4 dry chorizo or kielbasa sausages, or mild cooked sausage (about 12 ounces altogether), cut into ¼-inch dice

3 cups stone-ground yellow cornmeal

2¼ cups unbleached all-purpose flour

¾ cup whole-wheat flour

1 tablespoon baking powder

1½ teaspoons salt

3 tablespoons light brown sugar, packed

5 eggs

1½ cups sour cream

1½ cups milk

½ cup apple juice or cider

8 Red Delicious apples, peeled and cut into ¼-inch dice

Pinch of ground cumin

2 green onions, white and light green parts only, thinly sliced

1 tablespoon chopped chives

2 tablespoons unsalted butter, at room temperature

Rub the marinade all over the turkeys, cover, and refrigerate for at least 12 hours. Roast the turkeys in a preheated 350°F oven until done, about 5½ hours. Baste every half hour to hour with the beer. If one part of the turkey skin looks like it's getting too brown, simply cover it with a tent of foil. (To test for doneness, prick the skin at the thickest part of the thigh with a knife; the juices should run clear.) Let rest for about 20 minutes prior to carving.

Prepare the stuffing: Preheat the oven to 375°F. In a medium sauté pan over moderate heat, sauté the sausage until heated through and lightly browned. Set aside. In a large bowl, sift together the cornmeal and the flours (to keep it from getting lumpy). Stir in the baking powder, salt, and brown sugar. In a separate bowl, whisk together the eggs, sour cream, and milk. Add the wet ingredients to the dry, and mix until blended.

Add the apple juice. Stir in the chorizo, apples, cumin, green onions, and chives. Grease half a hotel pan (a 2-inch-deep, 12-by-12-inch baking pan) with the butter. Scrape the batter into the pan. Bake until the top is golden and a knife inserted in the center comes out clean, about 40 minutes. Let cool slightly; then cut into squares and serve at room temperature.

Arroz Moro

MAKES 12 TO 15 APPETIZER SERVINGS   Versions of arroz moro, also called Moros y Cristianos (Moors and Christians) because of the black beans and white rice, are a favorite in Cuba, Puerto Rico, and, of course, New York! A versatile party dish, it can be served with grilled *churrasco* (steak) or by itself. Plan to make this rice the day before you're going to use it; not only will you have it finished and ready to serve, but the flavor will also be *mucho mejor,* much better!

1 pound dried black beans, picked through and rinsed

About 2½ cups long-grain rice

1 tablespoon canola oil

1 tablespoon minced garlic

1 cup diced red onion

1 cup diced green onions, white and light green parts only

1 cup diced red bell pepper

1 tablespoon ground cumin

1 tablespoon chili powder

1½ teaspoons ground black pepper

Kosher salt

½ cup chopped cilantro

1 cup Sofrito (page 136)

2 very ripe (black) plantains, sliced on an angle and fried (see page 29)

1 ear of corn (or 1 cup frozen corn kernels), roasted (see page 134)

Place the beans in a stockpot and add water to cover by about 4 inches. Bring to a boil. Simmer, stirring once in a while, until tender, between 1 and 2 hours, depending on the age and size of the beans. Check the beans frequently to make sure they are continuously covered with about 4 inches of liquid. Once the beans are cooked, drain them, but make sure you save the broth because you'll use it to cook the rice. Set the beans aside for now.

: : *continued*

Measure the broth reserved from the beans. You'll probably have about 6 cups. Whatever amount you have, you should measure half that amount in rice. (For example, if you have 5 cups of broth, you'll use 2½ cups of rice.) Bring the broth to a boil, add the rice, and return to a boil. Immediately lower the flame (it's important to use a low flame here), and cover the pot. Cook until the rice is tender, 30 to 45 minutes, checking it after 30 minutes.

While the rice is cooking, heat the oil in a large sauté pan over medium heat. Add the garlic, red onion, green onions, and bell pepper, and cook until softened, a couple of minutes. Stir in the cumin, chili powder, black pepper, and salt to taste. Add the cilantro and sofrito and mix just until well blended. Stir in the plantains and corn kernels and set aside.

In a large bowl, combine the rice and cooked beans. Stir in the vegetable mixture. Refrigerate overnight (or for up to 3 days). Return to room temperature just prior to serving.

Grilled Stuffed Lobster with Avocado and Manchego Cheese

MAKES 4 SERVINGS   Though it's hard to imagine, there was a time—about 200 years ago—when lobsters were so abundant that they were considered a poor man's food. (In fact, they were fed to prisoners and indentured servants!) Since the middle of the last century, lobsters have been considered haute cuisine, and lobster lovers are quite passionate about this crustacean delicacy. The cooking method here may be considered typical, but the presentation is dazzling—as are the sweet flavors of the lobster, avocado, and manchego cheese, with just a touch of saffron aïoli. This meal can be prepared as your friends are sipping their cocktails and munching on appetizers.

1 ripe Hass avocado, peeled, pitted, and coarsely chopped

½ beefsteak tomato, coarsely chopped

½ red onion, minced

Juice of 1 lime

Kosher salt and freshly ground pepper

2 lobsters, 1¼ pounds each, blanched for 4 minutes, and claws cracked, cleaned, and split in half

½ cup grated manchego (or white Cheddar) cheese

¼ cup Saffron Aïoli (page 136)

Thinly sliced chives, for garnish

Preheat the oven to 350°F. Combine the avocado, tomato, red onion, lime juice, and salt and pepper to taste in a bowl. Scoop some of the mixture into each lobster half and place the halves in a baking dish. Place the meat from a claw on top of each lobster half. Top with the grated cheese. Bake in the oven for 6 to 8 minutes. Then place under the broiler for 2 minutes, or until the cheese is bubbling. Place on individual plates, and finish with a drizzle of aïoli and a sprinkle of chives. Serve immediately.

Crispy East Coast Oysters with Sweet Fufu and Saffron Aïoli

MAKES 24 FRIED OYSTERS, 6 APPETIZER SERVINGS   On a recent family trip to Miami, I was reintroduced to the wonders of oysters. Whether straight from the sea or batter-fried, oysters are inspirational. Here they're lightly fried and combined with another Miami favorite: *fufu*, a garlicky sweet plantain purée, found (by a variety of names) throughout the Spanish-speaking Caribbean. The result, as I'm sure you'll soon discover, is a combination that is super *sabroso*, very tasty. Light, elegant, and distinctive, this appetizer could play a starring role at any cocktail party.

FUFU

2 tablespoons canola oil

1 red onion, finely diced

¼ cup unsalted butter

2 sweet plantains, roasted (see page 139)

2 cups yellow or white *harina precocida* (instant cornmeal)

¼ cup all-purpose flour

1 teaspoon kosher salt

¼ teaspoon freshly ground black pepper

1 tablespoon ground cumin

1 tablespoon granulated garlic

24 Malpeque (or Blue Point) oysters

Canola oil for deep-frying

½ cup Saffron Aïoli (page 136)

Chopped chives for garnish

Prepare the *fufu*: Heat the canola oil in a medium sauté pan over medium heat. Add the red onion and slowly let it caramelize until golden, 5 to 7 minutes. Add the butter and plantains and remove from the heat. Using a fork or potato masher, smash the plantains with the onion mixture. Set aside and let cool to room temperature.

: : *continued*

Crispy East Coast Oysters with Sweet Fufu and Saffron Aïoli

Next, prepare the breading. In a large bowl, combine the cornmeal, flour, salt, black pepper, cumin, and granulated garlic. Use a fork to mix well. Scoop out the oysters and save the bottom half of the shells (you'll be using them to serve the oysters). Cover the oysters with the breading mixture to prepare them for frying.

In a deep, heavy pot or deep-fryer, heat 3 inches of oil to 350°F. Fry the well-coated oysters until golden, about 20 seconds. Remove and drain on paper towels.

To serve, arrange the shells on a platter, or on a bed of mesclun lettuce. Place a spoonful of *fufu* on each shell, followed by an oyster. Drizzle the aïoli on top, then garnish with the chives. Serve immediately.

Shrimp with Braised Garlic, Ají Amarillo, and Cilantro Sauce

MAKES 24 SHRIMP This is my interpretation of the classic Spanish appetizer *gambas al ajíllo*. Here I've incorporated a Nuevo Latino touch of *ají amarillo*, which adds flavor and just a light kiss of spark. I like to serve these with Pomegranate Margaritas (page 120), a nice Chilean cabernet sauvignon, or Aguila (Colombian beer).

2 tablespoons minced garlic

¼ cup olive oil

24 medium shrimp, peeled and deveined, tails left on

Kosher salt and freshly ground pepper

½ cup thinly sliced green onions, white and light green parts only

½ cup coarsely chopped plum tomatoes

3 cups bottled clam juice, chicken stock (page 128), or canned low-salt chicken broth

3 tablespoons chopped cilantro, plus additional for garnish

6 tablespoons unsalted butter, cut into chunks

½ teaspoon ground cumin

2 teaspoons *ají amarillo* (see page 138)

Preheat the oven to 300°F. Place the garlic in the center of a legal envelope–size piece of foil. Add a few drops of olive oil and gently mix. Wrap up the garlic, and cook in the oven until golden and softened, 8 to 10 minutes.

Heat the remaining oil in a large sauté pan over medium heat (if you don't have a pan that will fit all 24 shrimp, cook in 2 pans). Add the shrimp and sprinkle with salt and pepper. Stir in the garlic, green onions, tomatoes, clam juice, 3 tablespoons cilantro, butter, cumin, and *ají amarillo*.

Cook until the shrimp turn pink, about 2 minutes on each side. Remove the shrimp and continue cooking the sauce until it reduces and thickens slightly, 5 to 7 minutes.

Spread the sauce on a serving platter and arrange the shrimp on top. Serve immediately, garnished with the additional cilantro.

Palomino's Vegetable Paella

MAKES 12 TO 15 APPETIZER SERVINGS Paella means party! Not literally, of course, but it is one of my favorite party dishes. When we have wine tastings at the restaurants, I'll often have large platters of paella so that while guests are sipping wine, they can try small tapas-size dishes of this colorful and tasty rice dish. Although paella doesn't take too long to prepare, you can always make the rice ahead of time, as we do in my restaurants.

6 cups water

3 cups long-grain white rice, rinsed

2 pinches saffron threads

1 tablespoon plus 1 teaspoon canola oil

1 tablespoon minced garlic

2 cups diced plum tomatoes

2 cups diced green onions, white and light green parts only

1 cup dry-packed sun-dried tomatoes, soaked in hot water for 20 minutes, drained, and diced

¼ cup shiitake mushrooms, stemmed and coarsely chopped

1 cup julienned roasted red bell pepper (see page 135)

1 teaspoon ground cumin

Kosher salt and freshly ground pepper

½ cup pitted and halved kalamata olives

2½ cups chicken stock (page 128) or canned low-salt chicken broth

1 teaspoon unsalted butter

4 cups baby spinach

1 cup chopped roasted Vidalia onions (see page 135)

2 tomatoes, roasted (see page 135) and coarsely chopped

Bring the water to a boil in a heavy saucepan. Add the rice and saffron. Stir, bring to a simmer, and cover. Cook over low heat for 15 minutes, or until al dente. Set aside.

In a large sauté pan or *paellera* (paella pan), heat 1 tablespoon of the oil over medium heat. Add the garlic and cook for about 1 minute. Add the plum tomatoes, green onions, sun-dried tomatoes, mushrooms, and red peppers. Add the cumin, and salt and pepper to taste. Stir in the olives, followed by the cooked rice. Pour in 2 cups of the chicken stock, and let the paella mixture cook, uncovered, until the rice is cooked through but not mushy, 5 to 10 minutes. The mixture should not be soupy.

In a separate sauté pan over medium heat, heat the remaining teaspoon of oil with the butter. Add the remaining ½ cup chicken stock and bring to a boil. Add the baby spinach, and cook just until wilted.

Just before serving the paella, stir in the wilted spinach, roasted onions, and roasted tomatoes. Serve immediately.

Arroz Moro
de Mariscos con Coco

MAKES ABOUT 6 SERVINGS   When I introduced this entrée as a special in Pacífico, my customers raved! This dish—which has Spanish and Colombian roots—is a wonderful second to a ceviche appetizer.

2 cups dried black beans, picked over and rinsed

2 whole cloves garlic, peeled, plus 1 tablespoon minced garlic

3 bay leaves

2 tablespoons vegetable oil

8 littleneck clams, scrubbed

½ cup dry white wine

8 mussels, bearded and rinsed

1 cup chicken stock (page 128) or canned low-salt chicken broth

1 pinch saffron threads

4 large shrimp, peeled and deveined, tails left on

Kosher salt

1 tablespoon unsalted butter

½ cup fresh or thawed frozen corn

½ cup diced seeded plum tomato

½ cup thinly sliced green onions, white and light green parts only

½ cup julienned roasted red bell peppers (see page 135)

2 cups cooked long-grain white rice

1 cup toasted coconut (see page 137), plus additional for garnish

½ cup coconut milk

2 tablespoons cream of coconut

Place the beans in a stockpot and cover with water by 4 to 5 inches. Add the whole garlic and bay leaves and bring to a boil. Simmer, stirring once in a while, until tender, 1 to 2 hours. Check frequently to make sure the beans are well covered with water. Once the beans are cooked, drain, remove the garlic and bay leaves, and set aside.

Heat 1 tablespoon of the oil in a medium sauté pan over medium heat. Add the minced garlic and clams. Pour in the white wine, stirring the mixture; the wine will evaporate. Add the mussels (you add them second because they cook faster than the clams) and the chicken stock. Stir in the saffron threads. As soon as the clams and mussels start to open (after 8 to 10 minutes), remove them from the heat and set them aside.

Meanwhile, cook the shrimp. In a small sauté pan, heat the remaining 1 tablespoon of oil over medium heat. Salt the shrimp lightly before adding it to the pan. Sauté the shrimp until just cooked, 3 to 5 minutes; you don't want to overcook it (or the shellfish). Remove from the heat.

In a large sauté pan, heat the butter over medium heat. Add the corn, tomato, green onions, and roasted peppers. Add the rice and black beans and stir. Add the 1 cup toasted coconut and sauté for about 5 minutes. Stir in the coconut milk and cream; heat through. Transfer to a serving dish. Serve immediately topped with the shrimp, cooked clams and mussels, and additional toasted coconut.

Black Quinoa and Sweet Plantain Shrimp Salad

MAKES ABOUT 12 SERVINGS This great summer salad is delicious, healthy, and gorgeous. Quinoa, an ancient couscous-like grain, is not only jam-packed with protein, it's also got a nutty, delicate flavor that marries well with a variety of foods. Though I've used black quinoa here, I encourage you to try both white and red quinoa with this salad. Stuffing beefsteak tomatoes— either yellow or red—with the quinoa salad makes a beautiful presentation. This salad can be served warm or at room temperature, on a mesclun or arugula-lined platter.

12 perfectly ripe yellow or red medium-size
   beefsteak tomatoes

2 tablespoons canola oil

½ teaspoon minced garlic

6 medium-size shrimp, peeled and
   deveined

2 pinches ground cumin

Pinch of saffron threads

Kosher salt and freshly ground pepper

1 small red onion, diced

3 green onions, thinly sliced, white and
   light green parts only

3 red bell peppers, roasted (see page 135)
   and diced

1 handful cilantro leaves, coarsely chopped

2 cups cooked black (or white) quinoa
   (see page 140)

1 plantain, roasted (see page 139) and diced

About 1 cup chicken stock (page 128)
   or canned low-salt chicken broth

Preheat the oven to 300°F. First prepare the tomatoes so that you can use them to serve your salad. Using a sharp knife, slice off the tops of the tomatoes either flat or in a zigzag pattern; you'll need the tops later, so don't discard them. Using a spoon, scoop out the insides. (You may want to save them for a sauce or another salad.) Set aside.

: : continued

Black Quinoa and Sweet Plantain Shrimp Salad

Heat 1 tablespoon of the canola oil in a medium sauté pan over medium heat. Add the garlic and sauté for 1 minute. Add the shrimp, 1 pinch of cumin, a couple of saffron threads, and salt and pepper to taste. Sauté just until the shrimp starts to turn pink, about 3 minutes. You don't want to cook it all the way because you'll be cooking it more in the oven. Using tongs, remove the shrimp from the pan and, when cool enough to handle, dice into ¼-inch chunks. Clean the sauté pan with a paper towel.

Add the remaining tablespoon of canola oil to the sauté pan. Stir in the red onion, green onions, and bell peppers. Add the cilantro, the remaining saffron threads, and the remaining pinch of cumin and sauté over medium heat until the onion starts to soften, 3 to 5 minutes. Add the cooked quinoa, plantain, and diced shrimp and stir just to mix. Remove from the heat and transfer to a bowl.

Using a teaspoon, stuff the quinoa mixture into the prepared tomatoes. Set the tomatoes into a 1-inch-deep baking pan, cover them with their tops, and pour in the chicken stock so that it is about ¼ inch deep around the tomatoes. Bake until the tomato warms up, about 7 minutes. Transfer to a platter and serve.

Sonora Caesar and Anchovy Salad

MAKES 4 TO 6 SERVINGS   Even if you weren't a fan of anchovies before, these light and silver *boquerones*—Spanish white anchovies—may convince you otherwise! These anchovies, served often as appetizers in tapas bars throughout Spain, are much less salty and more delicate than the darker oil-packed version commonly sold in the United States. As long as you keep some white anchovies on hand, you can whip up this salad when unexpected guests arrive for a light lunch or late-afternoon cocktails.

6 white anchovies for the dressing, plus 4 for the salad

¼ cup white balsamic vinegar

½ cup canola oil

1 head romaine lettuce, hearts and tender leaves only, torn into 1-inch chunks

Kosher salt and freshly ground pepper

4 French Bread Croutons (page 131), crushed

Juice of ½ lemon

4 vine-ripened tomatoes, cut into quarters

Pinch of chopped chives

In a blender, combine 6 anchovies and the vinegar. Slowly drizzle in the oil and process just until blended. Set aside.

Place the torn lettuce in a large bowl. Add 4 anchovies. Season to taste with salt and pepper and toss to mix. Add the dressing and toss well. Top with the croutons and lemon juice. Add the tomatoes and chives and serve immediately.

Sugarcane Shrimp Skewers with Jalapeño Coconut Sauce

MAKES 24 SHRIMP   It's amazing that the jalapeño/coconut milk combination can be found in cultures as disparate as those of Jamaica and Thailand. After one taste, you'll also fall in love with this balanced combo of soothing soft coconut milk and the slight bite of jalapeño. This recipe is as perfect for fall barbecues as it is for spring or summertime ones (and you can use this marinade for chicken or beef, as well as for shrimp). Serve with Coconut Mojitos (page 122) or Mango Caipiroskas (page 124). If using wooden skewers, soak them in water for about 30 minutes.

MARINADE

3 tablespoons finely chopped cilantro

2 cloves garlic, minced

1 teaspoon ground cumin

½ teaspoon kosher salt

¼ teaspoon ground pepper

1 cup canola oil

24 medium-size shrimp, peeled and deveined, tails left on

SAUCE

2 stalks lemongrass, coarsely chopped

2 tablespoons cilantro

2-inch chunk of fresh ginger, peeled and coarsely chopped

2 shallots

2 cups dry white wine

2 cloves garlic, chopped

2 tablespoons coriander seed, crushed

1 tablespoon cumin seed

½ cup cream of coconut

One 14-ounce can coconut milk

Salt and freshly ground pepper

¼ teaspoon curry paste

4 jalapeño chiles, roasted (see page 135) and minced

24 two-inch slices of sugarcane, or wooden skewers (these can be longer)

Prepare the marinade: Combine the cilantro, minced garlic, cumin, salt, pepper, and oil in a bowl. Whisk together. Use immediately or cover and refrigerate for up to 3 weeks. When ready to use, add the shrimp and marinate in the refrigerator for no more than 1 hour.

Prepare the sauce: While the shrimp is marinating, in a medium saucepan over medium-high heat, combine the lemongrass, cilantro, ginger, shallots, white wine, garlic, coriander, and cumin seed. Reduce until almost dry, 5 to 6 minutes. Add the cream of coconut and the coconut milk and reduce by about a quarter, about 15 more minutes. Turn off the heat, strain, and return to the saucepan. Stir in salt and pepper to taste and the curry paste and jalapeños. Let cool to room temperature. Use immediately, or cover and refrigerate for up to 45 minutes.

Prepare a fire in an outdoor grill. You can also use a grill pan heated over high heat. Oil the grill or grill pan, if using. Thread the marinated shrimp on the skewers and grill until pink, about 3 minutes on each side. Serve hot or at room temperature, with the sauce alongside for dipping.

Marinated Lobster Tail and Scallop Pinchos

MAKES 12 SKEWERS The inspiration for this appetizer comes from my first trip to Acapulco, Mexico, where I traveled with my parents as a child. Our trip—which was replete with visual and culinary delights—included one evening of grilled lobster on the beach. The herb flavors in this interpretation certainly complement—and balance—the rich meat of the lobster and scallops. I recommend serving these *pinchos* (skewered seafood or meat) with Mango Caipiroskas (page 124).

6 lobster tails, blanched for 4 minutes, removed from the shell, and split in half

12 sea scallops

12 ten-inch wooden skewers

Leaves from 3 sprigs rosemary

Leaves from 15 sprigs thyme

¾ teaspoon sweet paprika

¾ teaspoon ground cumin

½ teaspoon granulated garlic

1 cup canola oil

Pinch of salt

Thread the lobster tails and scallops on the skewers, starting with a piece of the tail, then a scallop, and then the top of the tail. If using wooden skewers, soak them in water for about 30 minutes.

In a large bowl, whisk together the rosemary, thyme, paprika, cumin, garlic, oil, and salt. Place the skewers in the marinade, cover, and refrigerate for approximately 15 minutes.

Light a fire in a charcoal or gas grill. Remove the skewers from the marinade. Grill until fully cooked, 3 to 5 minutes on each side.

MAYBE IT'S BECAUSE I'VE GOT AN INCURABLE SWEET

chapter

6 Desserts

TOOTH, OR MAYBE IT'S BECAUSE I LIKE LEAVING A LASTING IMPRESSION—BUT the end of the meal is as important to me as the beginning! While a light sorbet can be as luscious as a passionate kiss, Semisweet Chocolate Churros, Mexican doughnuts sprinkled with sugar and chocolate, are just as heavenly. For those of you who are fans of chocolate and dulce de leche, Arlen's brownies may give you just what you desire. I suggest offering an assortment of desserts—which is what I do in my restaurants, at parties, and at home—so that your guests will leave with an even bigger smile than the one they walked in with.

Mango and Caipirinha Sorbet

MAKES 6 TO 8 SERVINGS Tropical-flavored sorbets are refreshing and palate cleansing. They can be served with heavier dessert fare, an assortment of cut fruit, or on their own. When serving dessert to a larger crowd, I often create platters of assorted treats, including one or two scoops of sorbet.

1 cup water

½ cup sugar, or according to taste

2 cups mango pulp (Alphonso mango pulp is ideal. If not already sweetened, add more sugar.)

1 cup fresh lime juice, plus strips of lime zest for garnish

¼ cup cachaça (Brazilian rum) or white rum

In a small saucepan, combine the water and sugar. Bring to a boil, lower the heat, and simmer until the sugar is dissolved. Remove from the heat and cool completely.

In a blender, combine the mango pulp with the lime juice. Add the cooled sugar water and cachaça. Blend until well mixed. Place in an ice cream maker and process according to the manufacturer's instructions. If not using an ice cream maker, place the chilled mixture in a stainless-steel or other metal baking pan, cover with plastic wrap, and freeze until softly set, about 2 hours. Transfer the partially frozen mixture to a food processor and process until smooth and fluffy, about 10 seconds. Return the mixture to the baking pan, freeze until half-set, and repeat the process. After the second blending, transfer it to a plastic container. To prevent ice crystals from forming, place a piece of plastic wrap directly on the surface of the sorbet before putting the lid on the container. Store in the freezer until the sorbet is solid, about 4 hours.

Remove the sorbet from the freezer 10 minutes before serving. Serve in chilled stemmed glasses. Garnish each serving with lime zest.

Sweet Corn Arepas Topped with Dulce de Leche Ice Cream

MAKES 6 SERVINGS This dessert is not only gorgeous and tasty, it's easy to prepare ahead of time. All you need—as far as tools go—is a 3-inch ring (which, as my chef de cuisine at Pacífico, Peter Cregan, suggests, if you're handy with a table saw, you can make by purchasing 3-inch PVC piping and cutting it into a 2-inch-high ring mold). Make these three-tiered napoleons and keep them in your freezer until about half an hour before serving. Then plate them, top with the Papaya-Mango Salsita, and serve.

AREPAS

2 cups fresh or thawed frozen corn kernels

1½ cups hot water

2 cups yellow *harina precocida* (instant cornmeal)

2 teaspoons sour cream

1 tablespoon sugar

6 tablespoons grated Cheddar cheese

2 tablespoons unsalted butter

PAPAYA-MANGO SALSITA

½ cup diced papaya

½ cup diced mango

¼ cup pineapple juice

1 tablespoon amaretto

1 teaspoon coarsely chopped mint leaves, plus additional leaves for garnish

2½ cups dulce de leche ice cream, or 2 cups vanilla ice cream and ½ cup Dulce de Leche (page 130), in a squeeze bottle

Prepare the *arepas*: In a blender, process the corn kernels and hot water until smooth.

Pour the *harina precocida* into a large bowl. Stir in the sour cream and sugar. Pour in the water-and-corn mixture while stirring with your hands or a wooden spoon. Add the grated cheese. Form the mixture into a ball, then divide it into 18 pieces. Roll each piece into a ball and flatten it into a pancake about ¼ inch thick and 3 inches in diameter (rub your fingers around the edge so that it maintains its thickness). At this point you can cover the *arepas* with a damp kitchen towel, and refrigerate them for up to 1 day before sautéing.

: : *continued*

Sweet Corn Arepas Topped with Dulce de Leche Ice Cream

Melt the butter in a medium sauté pan (or on a sandwich press) over medium heat. Sauté the arepas until golden, 3 to 5 minutes on each side. They should be toasted on the outside but soft in the middle. Let cool to room temperature.

Meanwhile, prepare the salsita: Combine the papaya, mango, pineapple juice, and amaretto in a bowl. Cover and refrigerate for up to 1 day. Stir in the mint leaves just before serving.

Assemble the desserts: Using a 3-inch ring mold, start with one *arepa,* followed by a scoop of ice cream. Smooth out the ice cream with a spoon. Add another *arepa* and another layer of ice cream. Top with a third *arepa.* Remove the ring, cover, and freeze. (I recommend freezing several in a sheet pan lined with parchment paper.)

Remove from the freezer approximately half an hour before serving. Top with the salsita and, if you're using vanilla ice cream, drizzle each one with dulce de leche. Garnish with mint leaves and serve.

Semisweet Chocolate Churros

MAKES 4 TO 6 SERVINGS Churros, Spanish doughnuts beloved throughout the New World, easily marry with so many flavors, from chocolate to fruit sauces. Although they are traditionally shaped with a *churrera,* a tool with a plastic or wooden plunger that extrudes the dough into its traditional fluted shape (which is key, or they'll turn out hard and doughy), I recommend spooning the mixture into a cake decorators' pastry bag with a ½-inch star tip (the kind used to decorate cakes). For variety, try drizzling them with a bit of Guava Sauce (page 132) or Dulce de Leche (page 130).

2 cups water

3 tablespoons unsalted butter

3 tablespoons granulated sugar, plus ½ cup for rolling

2½ cups all-purpose flour

Pinch of salt

2 eggs, at room temperature

Canola oil for deep frying

3 tablespoons unsweetened cocoa powder

In a medium saucepan over medium heat, combine the water, butter, and 3 table-spoons sugar. Bring to a boil, and cook, stirring constantly, until the butter is completely melted and the sugar is dissolved. Remove from the heat. Add the flour quickly, all at once. Using a sturdy whisk, stir until smooth. Add the salt. Let rest for 2 minutes. Then add the eggs, one at a time.

Heat 3 inches of oil in a deep, heavy pot to 375°F, or in a deep-fryer according to the manufacturer's instructions, until a piece of dried bread floats and turns golden in the oil after 1 minute.

Spread the remaining granulated sugar and unsweetened cocoa on a plate.

Spoon the batter into a churro maker or pastry bag. Squeeze five or six 3-inch lengths of the mixture into the hot oil, using a knife to slice off each length as it emerges from the nozzle. Cook the churros, in batches as needed, until golden. Quickly drain on paper towels and roll in the sugar mixture while still warm. Serve immediately.

Arlen's
Dulce de Leche Brownies

MAKES 24 BROWNIES   Anyone who knows my writer, Arlen, knows that she loves to bake. Served to an audience of her children and husband, their friends, her students (she's an English professor) and colleagues, and my restaurant staff, this variation on her usual straight-chocolate-brownie theme is quickly winning over both old and new fans. For larger crowds, Arlen suggests preparing one batch without nuts and one with toasted pecans or walnuts.

1¼ cups semisweet chocolate chips

½ cup butter, cut into pieces

3 eggs

1¼ cups flour

1 cup sugar

1 tablespoon pure vanilla extract

¼ teaspoon baking soda

1 tablespoon granulated instant espresso coffee

¼ cup Dulce de Leche (page 130), at room temperature

Preheat the oven to 350°F. Butter a 13-by-9-inch baking pan. In a medium saucepan over low heat, melt 1 cup of the chocolate chips with the butter. Stir until smooth and remove from the heat. Stir in the eggs, flour, sugar, vanilla, and baking soda. Add the instant espresso and mix well. Stir in the remaining chocolate chips. Scrape into the prepared pan and spread evenly. Using teaspoons full of dulce de leche, place dollops (about 4) around the pan of dough. Use a knife to swirl them around just a bit (as if you were making a marble cake). Bake for about 35 minutes, or until a toothpick inserted in the center comes out slightly sticky. Let cool slightly before cutting.

chapter

Cocktails

EXPERIENCE. IN MY RESTAURANTS, WE CONSTANTLY EXPLORE THE POSSIBILITIES OF cocktail flavors, thinking always about how certain tastes complement each other. Just as you might take the time to find a wine that enhances your dining experience, you should explore cocktail possibilities that do the same. From the slightly tart Pomegranate Margarita to the Amanda, a chocolate martini, find choices that stir your cocktail fantasies.

Pomegranate Margarita

MAKES 1 SERVING The ancient Egyptians had the right idea when they fermented pomegranates to make wine; the sparkling, sweet-tart flavor of this fruit is seductive in a number of different forms. Here it's combined with a classic margarita to create a refreshing cocktail that fits, whether or not pomegranates are in season!

1 ounce triple sec

2 ounces Cuervo Gold tequila

3 ounces pomegranate juice

Juice of ¼ lime (about ½ ounce)

Lime slice, for garnish

Fill a cocktail shaker with ice. Add the triple sec, tequila, pomegranate juice, and lime juice. Cover, shake, and strain into a glass. Serve immediately, garnished with the lime slice.

Pineapple Mojito

MAKES 1 SERVING An ice-cold Pineapple Mojito is an ideal thirst quencher because it's fresh and light. Serve these with the Sirloin Steak, Ají Amarillo, and Shiitake Mushroom Spring Rolls (page 75).

10 mint leaves

2 ounces coarsely chopped fresh pineapple

2 ounces white rum

1 ounce pineapple juice

2 ounces margarita mix

Splash of club soda

Sugarcane, for garnish

In a glass, combine the mint leaves and fresh pineapple. Using a pestle or the end of a wooden spoon, muddle the leaves with the pineapple. Fill the glass with ice. Add the rum, pineapple juice, and margarita mix. Cover, and shake. Strain into a glass, top with the club soda, garnish with sugarcane, and serve immediately.

Passion Fruit Caipirinha

MAKES 1 SERVING   Any visitor to Brazil will tout the virtues of their national drink, the caipirinha, traditionally made with plenty of juicy limes and cachaça, Brazilian rum. Even in the States, this cocktail is a guaranteed party starter. This version is especially *fabuloso* thanks to the tropical flavors of passion fruit.

1 lime, cut into 8 wedges

2 heaping teaspoons sugar, or to taste

1½ ounces cachaça (Brazilian rum), or white rum

2 ounces passion fruit nectar

½ ounce triple sec

Sugarcane, for garnish

In a glass, combine the lime wedges and sugar. Using a pestle or the end of a wooden spoon, mash the lime pieces to extract the juice and oil from the skin. Fill the glass with ice. Add the cachaça, passion fruit nectar, and triple sec. Cover and shake. Strain into a glass, garnish with the sugarcane, and serve immediately.

Apple Margarita

MAKES 2 SERVINGS   My customers have been singing the praises of this tangy but not too sweet margarita.

3 ounces Cuervo 1800 Reposado tequila

2 ounces apple liqueur

3 ounces margarita mix

Pour the tequila and apple liqueur into a cocktail shaker filled with ice. Add the margarita mix, cover, and shake. Strain into 2 wine glasses and serve.

Noches de Cartagena

MAKES 1 SERVING Even if I weren't Colombian, I would still boast the enchantment of the Caribbean port city, Cartagena de las Indias. Cartagena's soft, sultry evenings are hard to capture in a cocktail, but the flavors of our national liquor (*aguardiente*), along with those of passion fruit and coco, remind me of one of my favorite places in the world.

3 ounces passion fruit nectar

2 ounces aguardiente

1 teaspoon cream of coconut

1 teaspoon superfine sugar, or to taste

1 teaspoon Cointreau

Combine all the ingredients in a shaker filled with ice. Shake well, strain into a glass, and serve.

Coconut Mojito

MAKES 1 SERVING The sweet and sour flavors of this mojito remind me of the first time I enjoyed this Cuban cocktail in Colombia. I was in La Vitrola, a great restaurant in Cartagena. I'll never forget when the owner asked his thirsty bar crowd, "Mojitos anyone?" Of course, his question was met with a resounding yes!

10 mint leaves

Juice of ½ lime

2 ounces coconut rum

3 ounces margarita mix

Splash of club soda

Sugarcane, for garnish

In a glass, combine the mint leaves and lime juice. Using a pestle or the end of a wooden spoon, muddle the leaves with the juice. Fill the glass with ice. Add the rum and margarita mix. Cover and shake. Strain into a glass, add a splash of club soda, garnish with sugarcane, and serve immediately.

Brazilian Cosmopolitan

MAKES 2 SERVINGS   Brazil—the country that shares a border with almost every other South American country—is as vast in influence as it is in territory. This cocktail, currently quite popular at Pacífico, should be served with samba music in the background in order to create the full Brazilian ambience.

1 lime wedge (optional)

¼ cup granulated sugar for the glass rims (optional)

7 raspberries

Juice of ½ lime

1 teaspoon superfine sugar

2 ounces raspberry vodka

2 ounces margarita mix

If desired, moisten the inside and outside of the rims of 2 martini glasses with the wedge of lime, then pour the granulated sugar onto a small plate and gently roll the rims so that they are well coated.

In a bar glass, combine the raspberries, lime juice, and superfine sugar. Using a pestle or the end of a wooden spoon, muddle them together. Fill the glass with ice. Add the vodka and margarita mix. Cover, and shake. Strain into the 2 glasses, and serve immediately.

Mango Caipiroska

MAKES 1 SERVING Developed as a vodka variation on the caipirinha, this is another cocktail made with muddled fruit. This drink blends mango and fresh lime juice with vodka. It is one of our most popular special drinks at Sonora, where I suggest that guests combine it with a serving of Marinated Lobster Tail and Scallop Pinchos (page 107).

3 tablespoons diced fresh mango, plus a mango slice, for garnish

Juice of ½ lime

1 teaspoon superfine sugar

1 teaspoon mango purée

2 ounces vodka

2 ounces margarita mix

In a glass, combine the diced mango, lime juice, and sugar. Using a pestle or the end of a wooden spoon, muddle them together. Fill the glass with ice. Add the mango purée, vodka, and margarita mix. Cover, and shake. Strain into a glass, garnish with the mango slice, and serve immediately.

Watermelon Martini

MAKES 1 SERVING This is the perfect Valentine's Day cocktail. Make sure you serve it with some Colombian—or your favorite—chocolates (and excellent company, of course).

3 ounces Grey Goose, or your favorite vodka

1 ounce Marie Brizard watermelon liqueur

1 strip lemon zest, for garnish

Pour the vodka and watermelon liqueur into a cocktail shaker with ice. Cover and shake. Strain into a chilled martini glass. Garnish with the lemon zest and serve.

Amanda

MAKES 1 SERVING   This chocolate martini is named after one of the biggest chocolate fans I know: my daughter, Amanda. Though it will be a few years before she can indulge in alcohol, I've been inspired on numerous occasions to create chocolate delights in her name.

2 tablespoons shaved semisweet chocolate for the glass rim

3 ounces Captain Morgan rum

1 ounce Godiva chocolate liqueur

Evenly distribute the chocolate shavings on a small plate. Wet the rim of a chilled martini glass, and gently twist it into the chocolate shavings until the rim is evenly coated. Set aside.

Pour the rum and chocolate liqueur into a cocktail shaker with ice. Cover and shake. Strain into the prepared martini glass and serve immediately.

Basics

There are certain essentials that my restaurant kitchens—and my home kitchen—can't be without. These basics, which include pantry and refrigerator items as well as methods of cooking, are fundamental for preparing my style of cooking: Nuevo Latino with a Mediterranean flair. I recommend trying them all. After a bit of practice, I'm sure they'll be easily incorporated into your routine as well!

Ají Verde

MAKES ABOUT 1 CUP Drizzled on top of empanadas, or scooped up with chips, this avocado-based Colombian sauce is simple and tasty.

2 avocados, peeled, pitted, and sliced

Kosher salt

¼ cup finely chopped red onion

½ teaspoon chipotle purée (see page 138)

Juice of 1 lime

In a medium bowl, mash the avocados. Add salt to taste, onion, chipotle purée, and fresh lime juice. Stir to blend. Use immediately.

Black Rice

MAKES BETWEEN 3 AND 4 CUPS COOKED RICE This colorful rice is rich in flavor and color. It's as easy to prepare as its white cousin.

2 cups black rice (I use Chinese Forbidden Rice)

3½ cups water

Pinch of kosher salt

Bring the rice, water, and salt to a quick boil, cover, and lower the heat to a simmer for 30 minutes. Turn the heat off and let the rice sit for 10 minutes before using.

Chicken Stock

MAKES ABOUT 6 CUPS   A key ingredient in so many recipes, homemade chicken stock adds depth of flavor to everything it touches.

1 small free-range chicken (about
   3½ pounds), quartered

10 cups cold water

1 teaspoon kosher salt

1 large stalk celery with leaves,
   coarsely chopped

2 carrots, peeled and coarsely chopped

1 onion, coarsely chopped

1 bay leaf

1 bunch cilantro, stemmed and coarsely
   chopped

Cloves from 1 small head garlic, peeled

Rinse the chicken well and trim off all excess fat. Put it in a large stockpot and add the water. Add the salt and bring to a boil. Skim off any fat or scum that rises to the surface. Add the remaining ingredients and reduce the heat to low. Simmer until the chicken is fork-tender, about 2 hours, skimming occasionally as necessary. Add water as needed to keep the chicken covered.

Pour the stock through a fine-mesh strainer into another pot or large bowl, pressing on the solids with the back of a large spoon to release the liquid. Spoon off the fat that rises to the top. You can make the stock even clearer by straining it through paper towels. Let cool to room temperature. Transfer to airtight containers and refrigerate overnight. Store in the refrigerator for up to 3 days, or freeze for up to 3 months.

Chipotle Garlic Mayonnaise

MAKES 1 CUP   Technically a chipotle aïoli, this smoky mayonnaise will seduce you with its flavors and versatility. Add or subtract chipotle purée according to your own taste.

½ teaspoon minced garlic

1 teaspoon chipotle purée (see page 138)

1 cup mayonnaise

Combine the garlic, chipotle purée, and mayonnaise. Cover and refrigerate for at least an hour. Use immediately, or refrigerate for up to 2 weeks.

Chipotle Sour Cream

MAKES 1 CUP   In a heartbeat, chipotle jazzes up sour cream! Keep it in a squeeze bottle for topping off your quesadillas—or your roasted potatoes.

1 teaspoon chipotle purée (see page 138)

2 teaspoons roasted garlic (see page 135)

1 cup sour cream

Combine the chipotle purée, roasted garlic, and sour cream. Cover and refrigerate for at least an hour. Use immediately, or refrigerate for up to 2 weeks.

Coconut Mixture

MAKES ABOUT 1½ CUPS   As a young boy, I learned that many of my favorite coconut-enhanced dishes came from Cartagena, a gorgeous Caribbean city in Colombia. Today I've incorporated coconut, along with various spices, into many of my dishes. This mixture, used for both salsas and marinades, has the added spark of Thai spices.

1 cup white wine

1 small shallot, sliced

¼ cup chopped lemongrass

One 14-ounce can coconut milk

4 ounces cream of coconut

2 teaspoons Thai curry paste (available in specialty stores and Asian markets)

In a small saucepan over medium heat, combine the white wine, shallot, and lemongrass and bring to a boil. Simmer until almost dry, about 5 minutes. Stir in the coconut milk, cream of coconut, and Thai curry paste and bring to a boil again. Simmer for 15 minutes. Strain and use immediately, or cover and refrigerate for up to 1 week.

Dulce de Leche (Caramelized Milk)

Dulce de leche has been in my life ever since I can remember! Here are two recipes: one is the one my *abuelita* (grandmother) used, and the other is a less labor-intensive method.

Grandma's Dulce de Leche

MAKES ABOUT 2 CUPS

4 cups whole milk

2 cups sugar

¼ teaspoon baking soda

Pinch of ground cinnamon

In a large saucepan, combine all the ingredients. Cook over medium heat, without stirring, for 15 to 20 minutes. Reduce the heat to low and cook for 25 to 30 minutes, stirring constantly with a wooden spoon. When the mixture thickens so much that you can see the bottom of the pan as you stir, remove from the heat. Let cool completely. Cover and store in the refrigerator for up to 2 weeks.

Easy Dulce de Leche

MAKES 1¾ CUPS

One 14-ounce can sweetened condensed milk

Put the unopened can of sweetened condensed milk in a stockpot, and add cold water to cover by 2 inches. Bring the water to a boil and cook for 1 hour and 45 minutes. Check the water often to make sure it is always covering the can. Also, do not let it cook for more than 2 hours; not only will you overcook the dulce de leche, you will also run the risk of exploding the can (which, I am happy to report, has never happened in my family, though we have been making dulce de leche for many, many years). Using tongs, occasionally turn the can over to stir the milk.

Remove the can from the water and let cool completely before opening. Transfer the caramelized milk to an airtight container and store in the refrigerator for up to 2 weeks.

French Bread Croutons

MAKES ABOUT 14 CROUTONS   Easy to store and pull out at the last minute, these croutons are larger than the ones you may be familiar with. However, I find that this size can be used for spreading salsas, or for garnishing dishes such as Niçoise Olives and Goat Cheese, Lamb Anticucho Style (page 23). You can make them ahead and keep them in an airtight container for up to 1 week. For a garlic version, simply top pieces with a sprinkle of minced garlic and a drizzle of olive oil.

: : *continued*

1 baguette (French-style bread), sliced ¼ inch thick

Preheat the oven to 350°F. Place the bread rounds, in a single layer, on a baking sheet. Bake until they start to brown, 7 to 10 minutes. Turn them over and continue baking until that side is brown as well, several minutes more. Let cool to room temperature before serving or storing in an airtight container.

Guacamole

MAKES ABOUT 2½ CUPS   This chunky Mexican sauce is a great complement to so many dishes. With avocados readily available, I strongly suggest that you make your own (instead of purchasing it).

4 ripe Hass avocados, peeled, pitted, and coarsely chopped

1 medium red onion, diced

¼ cup chopped cilantro

1 teaspoon Tabasco sauce

1 teaspoon kosher salt

2 red beefsteak tomatoes, finely diced

Juice of ½ lemon

In a large glass or ceramic bowl, combine the avocados, onion, and cilantro and mix well. Add the remaining ingredients and stir until well blended. Serve immediately or cover tightly and refrigerate for up to 1 day.

Guava Sauce

MAKES ABOUT 1 CUP   This simple sauce can be drizzled on top of ice cream or churros (page 115).

¾ cup guava purée (available at Latin American and large supermarkets)

¼ cup water

In a small bowl, combine the guava purée and water and mix until blended. Put the sauce in a squeeze bottle. Use immediately, or store in the refrigerator for up to 1 week.

Lobster

Although in several recipes I've indicated that frozen and canned lobster meat can be substituted for fresh, I always prefer using the real thing! Once you've cooked lobster a couple of times, you'll agree that fresh is best (and that it's not too tough to make).

1 tablespoon whole black peppercorns

½ cup white wine

1 carrot, peeled

1 onion, peeled and cut into quarters

1 celery stalk

Kosher salt and freshly ground pepper

1 lobster, ¼ pounds

Bring a large pot of water to a boil over medium heat. Add the peppercorns, wine, carrot, onion, celery, and salt and pepper to taste and return to a boil. Add the lobster. Cook until you can see a gap between the tail and the body cavity and white foam from that area is visible, about 5 minutes (or 4 minutes per pound). Remove and immediately submerge in ice water. Use immediately, or cover and refrigerate for up 2 days.

Mango, Jalapeño, and Radish Salsita

MAKES ABOUT 3 CUPS This salsa, created to complement my Lobster Chipotle Crabcakes (page 16), can also be enjoyed on its own with chips.

2 mangos, peeled, pitted, and cut into ¼-inch dice

½ cup finely diced daikon (Japanese radish)

2 jalapeño chiles, roasted (see page 135), peeled, seeded, and diced

¼ cup mango nectar

2 tablespoons olive oil

¼ cup white balsamic vinegar

1 tablespoon chopped chives

In a large bowl, combine the mangos, daikon, jalapeños, and mango nectar. Stir well, using your hand or a wooden spoon. Stir in the olive oil and vinegar. Let sit for about 20 minutes, then stir in the chives and serve. Or cover and refrigerate for up to 2 days. Return to room temperature and stir in the chives just before serving.

Pepper Potato Chips

MAKES 8 TO 10 APPETIZER SERVINGS These sparky chips, kept on the bar at Pacífico, go well with just about anything!

Canola oil for deep-frying

4 Idaho potatoes, thinly sliced with a Japanese mandoline (or the slicing blade of a food processor, or a large chef's knife) and placed into cold water (which prevents them from oxidizing and helps prevent sticking)

2 teaspoons cayenne pepper

Kosher salt and freshly ground pepper

In a deep-fryer or heavy pot, heat 1 inch of oil to 300°F. Working in batches, gently add the potato slices (preferably one at a time to prevent sticking) to the hot oil and cook until browned on both sides, 2 to 3 minutes. Using a skimmer, transfer the potatoes to paper towels to drain. Sprinkle with the cayenne and salt and pepper to taste. Serve immediately, or store in an airtight container for up to 3 days.

Roasted Vegetables

Roasted vegetables are used in several of my recipes. This method of cooking enhances the natural flavors these foods already have.

Roasted beets: Preheat the oven to 350°F. Cut unpeeled beets into wedges. Lightly coat the beet wedges with olive oil and place them in an ovenproof pan. Sprinkle with salt and pepper. Cover with aluminum foil and bake for 45 minutes to 1 hour, or until tender. Let cool to room temperature, then peel.

Roasted corn: To roast ears of corn in the oven, I recommend leaving them in the husks. Remove the outer husks and the corn silk, and place the ears on the rack in a preheated 375°F oven for 15 to 20 minutes. To roast frozen corn kernels, thaw them and then toss them with vegetable or light olive oil and a bit of garlic in a very hot skillet until they are lightly browned. You can do the same with fresh corn kernels.

Roasted garlic: To roast single cloves of garlic in the oven, peel them, sprinkle them with a bit of kosher salt, and wrap them in foil. Place on a metal plate in a preheated 350°F oven for 12 to 15 minutes. To roast a whole head of garlic, remove any loose skin, wrap the garlic in foil, place on a baking sheet, and roast in a preheated 350°F oven for 45 minutes. The garlic will be roasted and tender. To remove, just squeeze the cloves out of the skin; mash to make paste.

Roasted tomatoes: To roast tomatoes in the oven, preheat the broiler. Core the tomatoes and then slice them in half lengthwise. Place on a broiler pan or sheet pan as close to the broiler as possible. Broil until browned and blistered all around, 6 to 8 minutes. When they are cool enough to handle, peel off the skin. Don't worry if it doesn't all come off—the charred skin adds a great flavor. You can achieve similar results by grilling the tomatoes for 8 to 10 minutes. (On a grill, however, keep the tomatoes whole and turn them with tongs.)

Roasted onions or shallots: Remove the outer, dry skin. Cut the onions or shallots in half. Coat the onions with olive oil, place on a baking sheet, and sprinkle with kosher salt. Roast in a preheated 350°F oven until lightly browned, about 45 minutes for onions or 15 to 20 minutes for shallots.

Roasted and peeled bell peppers and chiles: Spike a whole bell pepper (or chile) with a long fork and hold it directly over a gas flame, or place it on a grill over hot coals, or in a very hot cast-iron skillet. Turn the pepper until it is charred on all sides. Place in a plastic or paper bag and close the bag. Let sit for about 10 minutes, or until cool to the touch. Pull out the stem and rub off the black skin. Cut the pepper in half and remove the seeds with your hands—don't use water or you will lose all those wonderful oils you worked so hard to get. Use right away, or submerge in olive oil, cover tightly, and refrigerate for up to 3 days.

TO ROAST PEPPERS AND CHILES UNDER A BROILER: Cut the peppers (or chiles) in half lengthwise. Core them and remove the seeds and ribs. Lay the peppers, skin side up, on a baking sheet as close to the heat source of a preheated broiler as possible, and broil until the skins are charred. You may want to use kitchen gloves when dealing with hot chiles; if you have a small cut, those little seeds can burn.

Saffron Aïoli

MAKES ABOUT 1 CUP   Before I lived in France, I knew nothing of this fabulous garlic mayonnaise; now I can't imagine my life without it! This adaptation, which utilizes the earthy flavor of saffron, tastes terrific and looks gorgeous.

½ cup dry white wine

2 teaspoons minced garlic

Pinch of saffron threads

Kosher salt

1 cup mayonnaise

In a sauté pan over medium-high heat, combine the white wine and garlic. Add the saffron and salt to taste, and reduce by half, 5 to 7 minutes. Simmer for a few minutes, and then set aside to cool to room temperature.

Once cooled, stir the wine mixture into the mayonnaise. Cover and refrigerate for at least an hour, stir (you'll see how richly yellow the mayonnaise becomes!), and use immediately or refrigerate for up to 2 weeks.

Sofrito

MAKES ABOUT 1½ CUPS   Found in various forms throughout the Americas, this sauce can be used to thicken and flavor soups, dolloped on top of paellas, or served on its own to accompany a plate of golden yuca fries.

2 tablespoons olive oil

1 small onion, finely chopped

1 teaspoon mashed roasted garlic (see page 135)

3 ripe medium tomatoes, cut into ¼-inch dice

½ teaspoon ground cumin

⅓ cup finely chopped green onions, white and light green parts only

⅓ cup chopped cilantro

1 bay leaf

1 cup chicken stock (page 128), canned low-salt chicken broth, or water

Kosher salt and freshly ground pepper

Heat the oil in a medium, heavy saucepan over medium heat and sauté the onion and garlic for 1 minute. Add the tomatoes, cumin, and green onions. Sauté until the onions become translucent, about 2 minutes. Add the cilantro, bay leaf, chicken stock, and salt and pepper to taste, and simmer for 7 to 10 minutes. Use immediately, or let cool, cover, and refrigerate for up to 1 week. You can also freeze this sauce for up to 6 months and thaw just prior to using. Stir well before serving.

Sun-Dried Tomato Chimichurri

MAKES ABOUT 1½ CUPS After customers order at Pacífico, they're served thick, warm slices of fresh-baked bread and a small dish of this sun-dried tomato chimichurri; both are consumed almost immediately! As a dip, a steak topping, or even a pasta sauce, this flavorful combination will delight you and your guests.

½ cup dry-packed sun-dried tomatoes, soaked in hot water for 20 minutes and drained

½ cup white balsamic vinegar

5 cloves roasted garlic (see page 135)

1 cup olive oil

Kosher salt and freshly ground pepper

In a blender or food processor, combine the tomatoes, vinegar, roasted garlic, and olive oil, and process until well blended. Sprinkle with salt and pepper to taste. Let sit for about 20 minutes, and serve. Or cover and refrigerate for up to 3 days. Return to room temperature before serving.

Toasted Coconut

MAKES ABOUT 2 CUPS Once you toast coconut for the first time, you'll start looking for ways you can use it! From salsas to cookies, toasted coconut is a versatile and tasty addition.

One 1-pound bag sweetened flaked coconut

Preheat the oven to 350°F. Pour the coconut flakes onto a sheet pan, making sure they're spread evenly. Bake until the edges brown, about 7 minutes. Stir and cook until uniformly golden brown, about 5 more minutes. The coconut cooks very quickly, so make sure you keep your eye on it.

Glossary of Ingredients

Some ingredients in *Fiesta Latina* may be new to you; this glossary will give you the pronunciation for and a brief description of the less familiar ingredients called for in these recipes. Please note that some fruit and vegetable names in Spanish vary depending on the region.

AGUARDIENTE (*ah-guahr-DIEN-tay*), Colombia's national liquor, is an anise-flavored brandy made from sugarcane syrup. It can usually be found in large liquor stores. If you can't find it, the Greek liquor ouzo is an acceptable substitute.

AJÍ AMARILLO (*ah-HEE ah-mah-REE-yo*) is a spicy yellow chile used throughout Peru in many of their national dishes. It can be found in dried, ground, frozen, or paste form in Latin American markets or through mail order. I recommend using the paste form (sold in jars) for these recipes.

ANNATO POWDER is made from ground achiote seeds, native to Central America and the Caribbean. This rust-colored powder, used throughout Latin America, adds a natural coloring and earthy flavor to all kinds of dishes, savory and sweet.

CACHAÇA (*kah-CHA-hsa*), Brazil's national liquor, and the main ingredient in the famous Brazilian cocktail caipirinha, is rum made from sugarcane. If cachaça is unavailable, light rum can be used as a substitute.

CHIPOTLES (*chee-POHT-layz*) are ripened and smoked jalapeño chiles. These fiery hot Mexican chiles enhance many dishes with their fabulous smoky flavor. Chipotles are most often found in cans (chipotles en adobo) in Mexican and other Latin American markets, preserved in a vinegar and tomato sauce. To make chipotle purée, empty a can of chipotles en adobo into a blender or food processor and blend until smooth. Cover and store in the refrigerator for up to 6 months. One 13½-ounce can of chipotles en adobo makes about 10 ounces chipotle purée.

CREMA AGRIA (*CRAY-mah AH-gree-ah*) is similar to a spicy sour cream and is used in a variety of Latin American dishes as both a topping (such as with soups and quesadillas) and an ingredient (as in my Chipotle Potato Cheese Gratin). It can be found in Latin American markets.

GUAVA (*GWAH-vah*) is a sweet tropical fruit now grown in parts of the United States. There are many varieties, but typically they are oval shaped and about the size of a small apple. Though fresh guavas may be difficult to find, guava juice, jelly, paste, and marmalade are available in Latino markets and large supermarkets.

HARINA PRECOCIDA (*ah-Ree-nah pray-koh-SEE-dah*), also called *masarepa* (*mah-sa-RAY-pah*), is precooked cornmeal used to make Colombian corncakes (*arepas*) and empanadas. This cornmeal, which is substantially more elastic than other cornmeals, can be found in Latin American markets or through mail order. I use the Venezolana brand.

JALAPEÑOS (*hah-lah-PAY-nyos*) are probably the most common of the fresh green chiles. Named after Jalapa, the capital of Veracruz, Mexico, they're small (2 to 3 inches long) and usually quite *picante,* or hot. Fresh jalapeños have a smooth, dark green skin and white seeds. They can be found in most large supermarkets.

PANELA (*pah-NAY-lah*), also known as *piloncillo* (pee-lon-SEE-yoh), is hardened brown cane sugar sold in loaves throughout Latin America. It has the consistency of very hard dark brown sugar and can be easily grated. Panela can be found in Latino markets and through mail order. Dark or light brown sugar can be used as a substitute.

PLANTAINS, or *plátanos* (*PLAH-tah-nos*), have long been an important ingredient in Latin American cooking. These cooking bananas can be eaten at all stages of ripeness, from unripe green to yellow to fully ripe or black. They look like overgrown

bananas and can now be found in most large supermarkets. To sauté ripe (black) plantains, dice them and sauté in 1 teaspoon of canola oil over medium heat until they start to caramelize, 5 to 7 minutes. To roast, preheat the oven to 450°F. Coat a baking sheet with canola oil or nonstick spray. Cut each plantain on the diagonal into ½-inch-thick slices. Brush the tops of the plantains with oil (or nonstick spray). Bake, turning occasionally, until the plantains are golden brown and tender, about 12 minutes.

POBLANOS (*poh-BLAH-nos*) are dark green (sometimes almost black) fresh chiles with a rich flavor. While some poblanos are mild, others are quite spicy. They're about 4 inches long and 2½ to 3 inches wide. Now grown in the United States, they are available in large supermarkets.

QUINOA (*KEY-noh-ah*), a grain now found in most supermarkets and natural food stores, was a staple of the Incas. Similar in appearance to couscous, it is a tiny, ivory-colored, bead-shaped grain with a delicate, nutty flavor. Quinoa is considered a complete protein because it contains all eight essential amino acids. To prepare quinoa, rinse it using a mesh strainer or by running fresh water over it. Drain off the excess water. Place in a saucepan and add water (2 cups water to 1 cup quinoa) and salt to taste and bring to a boil. Cook until al dente, about 10 minutes. You'll see that the grains have turned from white to transparent and the spiral-like germ has separated.

YUCA (*YOO-kah*), also called manioc, looks like a long, thick root (usually between 6 and 20 inches in length, and 2 to 3 inches in diameter) covered in a smooth (often waxed) dark brown, barklike skin, which is peeled to reveal a crisp white flesh. This root is used to make tapioca as well as flour, and is used in a number of Brazilian and Caribbean dishes.

Index

Table of Equivalents

The exact equivalents in the following tables have been rounded for convenience.

LIQUID/DRY MEASURES

U.S.	Metric
¼ teaspoon	1.25 milliliters
½ teaspoon	2.5 milliliters
1 teaspoon	5 milliliters
1 tablespoon (3 teaspoons)	15 milliliters
1 fluid ounce (2 tablespoons)	30 milliliters
¼ cup	60 milliliters
⅓ cup	80 milliliters
½ cup	120 milliliters
1 cup	240 milliliters
1 pint (2 cups)	480 milliliters
1 quart (4 cups, 32 ounces)	960 milliliters
1 gallon (4 quarts)	3.84 liters
1 ounce (by weight)	28 grams
1 pound	454 grams
2.2 pounds	1 kilogram

LENGTH

U.S.	Metric
⅛ inch	3 millimeters
¼ inch	6 millimeters
½ inch	12 millimeters
1 inch	2.5 centimeters

OVEN TEMPERATURE

Fahrenheit	Celsius	Gas
250	120	½
275	140	1
300	150	2
325	160	3
350	180	4
375	190	5
400	200	6
425	220	7
450	230	8
475	240	9
500	260	10